YORK NOTES

The Withered Arm and other Wessex Tales

Thomas Hardy

Note by Carolyn Mitchell

D0242502

 Longman

 York Press

YORK PRESS
322 Old Brompton Road, London SW5 9JH

PEARSON EDUCATION LIMITED
Edinburgh Gate, Harlow,
Essex CM20 2JE, United Kingdom
Associated companies, branches and representatives throughout the world

First published 1999

ISBN 0-582-38200-9

Designed by Vicki Pacey
Illustrated by Gerry Grace
Map by Gay Galsworthy
Phototypeset by Gem Graphics, Trenance, Mawgan Porth, Cornwall
Colour reproduction and film output by Spectrum Colour
Produced by Addison Wesley Longman China Limited, Hong Kong

ONTENTS

PREFACE

York Notes are designed to give you a broader perspective on works of literature studied at GCSE and equivalent levels. We have carried out extensive research into the needs of the modern literature student prior to publishing this new edition. Our research showed that no existing series fully met students' requirements. Rather than present a single authoritative approach, we have provided alternative viewpoints, empowering students to reach their own interpretations of the text. York Notes provide a close examination of the work and include biographical and historical background, summaries, glossaries, analyses of characters, themes, structure and language, cultural connections and literary terms.

If you look at the Contents page you will see the structure for the series. However, there's no need to read from the beginning to the end as you would with a novel, play, poem or short story. Use the Notes in the way that suits you. Our aim is to help you with your understanding of the work, not to dictate how you should learn.

York Notes are written by English teachers and examiners, with an expert knowledge of the subject. They show you how to succeed in coursework and examination assignments, guiding you through the text and offering practical advice. Questions and comments will extend, test and reinforce your knowledge. Attractive colour design and illustrations improve clarity and understanding, making these Notes easy to use and handy for quick reference.

York Notes are ideal for:
- Essay writing
- Exam preparation
- Class discussion

The author of this Note, Carolyn Mitchell, is a senior examiner for a major GCSE examination board in English and English Literature. She teaches English at a large comprehensive school in North Devon.

The text used in this Note is the 1984 Heinemann New Windmill edition.

Health Warning: **This study guide will enhance your understanding, but should not replace the reading of the original text and/or study in class.**

PART ONE

INTRODUCTION

HOW TO STUDY A SHORT STORY

You have bought this book because you wanted to study a collection of short stories, or an individual story, on your own. This may supplement work done in the class.

- You will need to read each story you are studying several times. Start by reading the story quickly for pleasure, then again slowly and carefully. Further readings will generate new ideas and help you to memorise the details of the story.

- Make careful notes on the themes, plots and characters you come across. Can you spot any themes which occur in more than one story?

- How is the story told? Is it narrated by one of the characters or by an all-seeing (omniscient) narrator who sees into the minds and motives of these imaginary beings?

- Which characters do you like or dislike? Why?

- A short story is different to a novel in lots of ways other than its length. Consider why the author might have chosen to use this method of writing, and how else it differs from other genres.

- Short stories need to have a strong beginning and end to contain the central idea or event. Which stories do this particularly well? Do you like or dislike any particular beginnings or endings?

- Some of the stories are very long, whilst some are very short indeed. Do you think that authors consider the length of their story to be important? What would be gained or lost from making them longer or shorter?

Studying on your own requires self-discipline and a carefully thought-out work plan in order to be effective. Good luck.

THOMAS HARDY'S BACKGROUND

Class divisions and barriers play an important part in many of Hardy's novels and short stories.

Thomas Hardy was born in 1840 at Higher Bockhampton, a hamlet near Dorchester in Dorset. He was the eldest son of Thomas Hardy, a stonemason, and Jemima Hardy, who had worked as a cook prior to her marriage. In later years Thomas Hardy felt almost ashamed of his parents due to their low social class and lack of education. He attended a school established by Julia Martin, the wife of the wealthy local estate owner. Mrs Martin was very fond of the young Thomas Hardy, and he became her favourite pupil. In return for her indulgence of him, he painted pictures for her.

Thomas's mother had ambitious plans for her son, and in 1849 she sent him to a school in Dorchester, which meant a six-mile walk for him each day. Thomas Hardy's horizons were broadened by the difference between country hamlet and county town. He had been a passionate reader from an early age, and Dorchester provided lots of opportunities for him educationally in terms of libraries and bookshops as well as school. Thomas Hardy was also a keen fiddle player, taking after his father, who was regularly asked to play at local events such as weddings and dances. He often accompanied his father to such festivities, enjoying the dancing and the hectic atmosphere.

At the age of sixteen, Thomas Hardy became an architect's apprentice in Dorchester. This was a significant achievement for the son of a craftsman. In his new position he found intellectually stimulating company, and he began to try his hand at writing verse. He continued to read avidly, and studied Greek and Latin. One friend who influenced Thomas Hardy was Horace Moule, and with Moule as his mentor, Hardy continued his self-improvement.

In 1862 Thomas Hardy decided to move to London. There he would be able to pursue a career as an architect as well as his literary interests. Through acquaintances, he found a post with the architect Arthur Blomfield. The social circle in which Thomas Hardy now found himself was very different to his previous experiences – for the reserved Thomas Hardy, the sophistication of his new colleagues seemed to be from a different world. He spent many hours at the International Exhibition of 1862, finding the art galleries particularly fascinating. During his travels around London he witnessed the great divide between the affluent and the impoverished, on a greater scale than he had previously known. Thomas Hardy's own social status was improving, and he moved to Paddington, an area of London that was the home of many professional people.

The differences between rich and poor are explored in many of Thomas Hardy's works.

In London, Thomas Hardy's health began to suffer, and in 1867 he returned to Dorset. His former employer, John Hicks, needed an assistant and so Thomas Hardy worked with him on church restoration. Thomas Hardy had literary ambitions and completed his first novel, *The Poor Man and the Lady*, in 1868. He approached several publishers but they all turned it down. Despite rejection, Thomas Hardy remained determined to become a successful writer. In 1870 Hicks sent him to North Cornwall to survey an old church in need of restoration. Whilst in Cornwall, Thomas Hardy met his future wife, Emma Gifford. At this time he was also writing *Desperate Remedies*, which became his first published novel.

Many writers found serialising their novels in magazines a lucrative means of publication.

Far from The Madding Crowd was published in serial form in the *Cornhill* magazine in 1873; this proved to be Thomas Hardy's first major success. The following year he married Emma Gifford. Hardy distanced himself from his family, finding his own origins a source of social embarrassment. In 1888 Hardy's first collection of short stories, *Wessex Tales*, was published.

In his later novels **characters** struggle against class divisions and expectations – *The Return of the Native* (published 1878), for example, explores this **theme** (see Literary Terms). In *Tess of the d'Urbervilles* (published 1891) the heroine comes from a poor family with social aspirations, and her tragedy seems to be predestined. Readers were shocked by this story, which includes the rape of the heroine, Tess, and concludes with Tess being hanged for the murder of her husband. The public outcry over this novel was surpassed by the scandal caused by the publication in 1896 of *Jude the Obscure*, in which the central characters have an illicit affair. Thomas Hardy began to devote himself to writing poetry after the public indignation and hostility aroused by these major novels.

In November 1912 his wife Emma died, and after her death Thomas Hardy wrote a series of love poems. He married again in 1914, continuing to write verse until his death in 1928. His ashes are buried in Westminster Abbey, and his heart is buried in the grave of his first wife, Emma, in Dorset.

CONTEXT & SETTING

Wessex

Thomas Hardy uses the rural south-western region of England as the setting for many of his novels and short stories. In Anglo-Saxon times this area was known as Wessex, and this is the name Thomas Hardy used in his fiction (see Map on p. 12 of this Note). All of the short stories in this collection are set in Wessex (although much of *The Son's Veto* is set in suburban London). The characteristic features of the area are reflected in the short stories: small, rural communities living in isolated locations, earning a living through conventional means.

Social class   English society in the 1800s was dominated by rigid class distinctions and social barriers. The lower classes were relatively uneducated and poor, providing unskilled labour; above these were skilled craftsmen. It is from these classes that Thomas Hardy draws many of his characters – they generally have a natural friendliness and possess down-to-earth wisdom. The upper classes and the aristocracy were educated and rich, often due to inherited land and wealth; these classes included religious figures, squires and other landowners. Upper-class characters in the short stories are usually less friendly and tend to be concerned with behaving appropriately in the eyes of society. Thomas Hardy uses the remote communities of fictional Wessex to provide readers with a **microcosm** (see Literary Terms) of the society at that time.

Rural life   The isolated locations of rural England produced close-knit, introspective communities in which generations of families lived. People would know each other's family history and the events of each other's lives. When people moved out of a community it would often be to avoid social disapproval and censure (as in *The Withered Arm* and *The Son's Veto*, for example). In these short stories it is generally the lower classes who are the most forgiving and the least self-righteous when it comes to judging the behaviour of others.

In Thomas Hardy's Wessex stories we encounter characters who earn their living as labourers, blacksmiths, publicans and shop owners; we also encounter a few smugglers and a variety of religious figures. All of these occupations are typical of such communities at that time. Members of the clergy – preachers, parsons, vicars and ministers – were a central part of the community, although being of a higher class than most of their congregation meant their strict moral codes were often not adhered to by the lower classes, who tended to formulate their own more expedient standards of behaviour. Thomas Hardy presents the religious figures in these short stories as either remote and severely judgemental, or as ridiculous and naïve. He believed that the moral standards of the Church were not upheld by members of the clergy even though their position in society allowed them to assume moral and social superiority. Witchcraft and witches were as real to these rural communities as the Church and clergy.

Distractions from the physically demanding lifestyle of many of the lower classes came about through celebrating Christian festivals and occasions. Weddings, funeral wakes and Christmas were occasions for the whole community to come together to eat, sing and dance. Local people would play instruments and sing in the choir, as described in *Absent-mindedness in a Parish Choir*. Thomas Hardy recognises the importance of religious institutions in this context and the characters in the short stories are seen to enjoy Christian festivities as social occasions, even if the Church did not necessarily approve of the manner of celebration. Another form of entertainment was recounting stories, and the personal **narrative** style of *Tony Kytes, the Arch-Deceiver* and *Absent-mindedness in a Parish Choir* creates the sense of an amusing **anecdote** (see Literary Terms) being recollected between friends.

Social conventions

Living in isolated communities meant that people seldom travelled far from the place where they were born. Travelling would have meant walking long distances for the majority of people, though horses and carts were available to transport produce to markets. Keeping horses and carriages was only for the rich, hence options were often limited when it came to learning a trade or marrying. In these short stories we encounter many characters who face dilemmas about marriage (for example in *The Son's Veto* and *The*

Melancholy Hussar of the German Legion). Society frowned upon marriages between upper and lower classes and this forced people to repress their feelings in favour of choosing an appropriate spouse. Behaviour according to the conventions of society was essential to gain approval. Thomas Hardy presents these conventions as restrictive and destructive in his short stories. Again it is the lower classes who feel less compelled to behave according to conventions, or who suffer passively due to them. All of the short stories in this collection comment in some way on social class and appropriate behaviour.

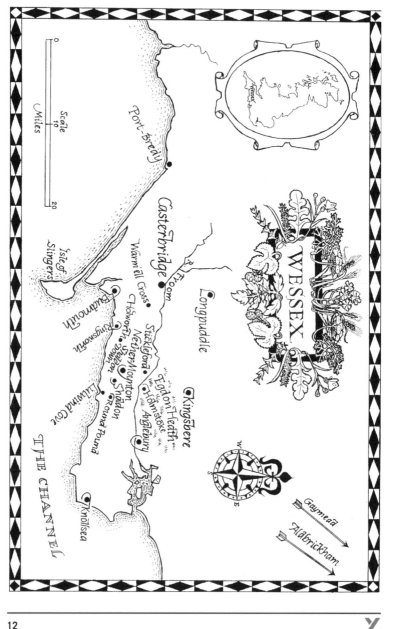

PART TWO

SUMMARIES

THE WITHERED ARM

DETAILED SUMMARY

A Lorn Milkmaid	The story begins with a conversation between a group of women milking cows one evening. They are gossiping about the return of the local landowner, Farmer Lodge, and his new bride. We learn that in the past Farmer Lodge had a relationship with Rhoda Brook, who is also milking the cows, though she does not take part in the conversation. When their work is finished, Rhoda Brook meets her son and tells him the news she has heard that evening: his father is married. Rhoda is curious to learn all she can about Farmer Lodge's new wife, and she commands her son to go and look at the bride on her way to her new home.
The Young Wife	As planned, Rhoda's son encounters Farmer Lodge and his young wife on the road to their village of Holmstoke (see Map of Wessex). He stares at her in order to be able to give his mother a detailed description. The young wife comments to her husband on how much the boy stared at her, and he changes the subject. Rhoda is anxious to know every detail from her son; but since the woman was sitting down when he saw her he could not tell whether she was taller than his mother or not. Rhoda sends her son to the church the next day to look at the woman again. He returns with new details of her appearance, and has concluded that Farmer Lodge's new wife is 'rather short' but very pretty.
A Vision	Two or three weeks after the homecoming of the newlyweds, Rhoda is becoming obsessed with the picture she has painted in her mind of the young wife,

made up from details given by her son, and from
comments she has overheard in the milking barn. One
night, she is haunted by this image in a nightmare in
which an apparition of the wife sits upon Rhoda's chest,
almost suffocating her. In a desperate effort, Rhoda
grabs the apparition's left arm and throws it backwards
from her.

The next day Rhoda is still deeply disturbed by the
seemingly life-like nature of the nightmare, when the
young wife visits Rhoda and her son with a charitable
gift of new boots for the boy. Having met Mrs Lodge
in person, Rhoda feels ashamed of her former thoughts.
When asked about her health, Mrs Lodge tells Rhoda
of her 'little ailment': her painful and bruised left arm.
Rhoda learns that the unexplained injury occurred on
the same night that she had been visited in her dreams
by the apparition and grabbed its left arm. She feels
guilty and wonders whether she has supernatural
powers and through them has caused Mrs Lodge's
mysterious injury.

A Suggestion   Rhoda's concern for Mrs Lodge's arm leads her to walk
near the outskirts of Holmstoke in the hope of meeting
her (we learn from the **narrator** (see Literary Terms)
that her first name is Gertrude). It is with some alarm
that Rhoda sees that the arm is causing Gertrude great
pain and has become shrivelled. Rhoda believes she can
detect her own handprint on the arm, while Mrs Lodge
confides in Rhoda that the appalling appearance of her
arm has made her husband love her less. Mr Lodge has
suggested that a witch or the devil may be responsible
for the injury.

When the two women meet again the next day,
Gertrude has been told by the locals about a man who
may be able to reveal the cause of her injury. She asks
Rhoda for more details about the man, named Trendle,

and is shocked to find out that he is a conjuror, or magician. Two days later she is desperate enough to consult even a conjuror about her arm, and she persuades Rhoda to take her to him.

Conjuror Trendle

The two women walk across the moor to Conjuror Trendle's house. He pronounces that the injury has been inflicted by 'an enemy', meaning it has been caused by witchcraft. He concocts a simple spell which reveals to Gertrude the identity of her enemy, while Rhoda waits outside, unable to see what is happening.

Gertrude is pale when she leaves Conjuror Trendle's house and her attitude towards Rhoda is no longer friendly. A rumour begins to circulate amongst the locals that Rhoda is responsible for the condition of Mrs Lodge's arm. Within a few months Rhoda and her son leave the area.

A Second Attempt

Six years later the Lodges' marriage has become strained due to the disfigurement of Gertrude's arm. She has tried every kind of cream and remedy to restore the arm, but nothing has worked. In desperation she visits Conjuror Trendle again. She begs him to use his magic to cure her arm, but he concedes it is beyond his powers. In order to cure her arm forever, he tells her, she must lay the limb on the freshly broken neck of a hanged man.

A Ride Gertrude becomes obsessed with this prospect of a cure, and she longs for someone to be hanged. Whilst her husband is away from home she learns of an impending execution in Casterbridge (see Map of Wessex). The relationship between Gertrude and her husband has worsened, and she reveals nothing of her plans, going to great lengths to conceal her journey to the county town.

A Water-side Hermit On arriving in Casterbridge, Gertrude visits the hangman to ask him to help her carry out the cure. They chat about the young man to be hanged and Gertrude is informed that he is not guilty of any crime, but is being hanged as a deterrent to others. The executioner agrees to help her.

A Rencounter Gertrude waits anxiously in the jail whilst the hanging takes place. She is determined to carry out the cure. With the help of the hangman she lays her arm on the corpse's neck. As she is doing this another woman's scream fills the room. Gertrude turns to see Rhoda Brook and her own husband. She realises that the dead young man is their son and she faints. She dies three days later.

Farmer Lodge sells his property and moves out of the area, and he dies two years later. Rhoda disappears for some time, but eventually returns to her home village and lives a simple life as a milkmaid again.

COMMENT This story examines rejection and the destructive forces of vanity and repressed jealousy. The effects of these are exacerbated by the setting: a small rural community in which witchcraft is believed to exist.

The previous relationship between Farmer Lodge and Rhoda Brook is alluded to early in the story. We

conclude that the relationship was not 'appropriate' –
Farmer Lodge is evidently a wealthy landowner
belonging to a higher class than Rhoda Brook – but
there seems to be some sympathy for Rhoda's situation
amongst the locals. She has been rejected by Lodge,
having borne him a son, and he has now married a
more suitable woman in terms of class – 'A lady

Consider what the
description of
Rhoda's house tells
us about her way
of life (see also
Language &
Style).

complete' (p. 5). The contrast between the affluent
lifestyle of Farmer Lodge and the impoverished lifestyle
of Rhoda and her son serves to emphasise the fact that
they are from different social backgrounds. Given that
the rejection seems likely to have been the result of class
prejudice, Thomas Hardy establishes in the first part of
the story a sense of foreboding about what will happen
when Farmer Lodge brings his new wife home.

Thomas Hardy creates **sympathy** (see Literary Terms)
for Rhoda early in the story. She avoids the gossip of
the locals concerning the new Mrs Lodge, and she is
shielded from it by the dairyman who tells them to get
on with their work. She satisfies her curiosity through
the details related to her by her son, who is **ironically**
(see Literary Terms) the first and last person to bring
the two women into contact. Thomas Hardy conveys
Rhoda's gradually increasing obsession with Mrs Lodge
through the plans for her son to observe the new wife.
We increasingly suspect that Rhoda is suppressing her
feelings towards the new Mrs Lodge – for example, she
seems satisfied when she discovers Mrs Lodge is short.
Her obsession with Mrs Lodge culminates in the
nightmare. The juxtaposition of this incident with Mrs
Lodge's visit to Rhoda's home heightens the tension in
the story, and the revelation of the injury immediately
implicates Rhoda as the perpetrator.

Thomas Hardy draws upon the belief in witchcraft to
create a sense of mystery surrounding powers beyond
the control of the characters and to heighten the

tension in the story. It is Rhoda's rejection by Farmer
Lodge that caused her to live at a distance from the
local community. People choosing to live in isolation,
especially women, were often believed to be witches,
and we learn that Rhoda has been 'slyly called a witch'
(p. 11) by the locals. Conjuror Trendle is also an
isolated character and is believed to have 'powers other
folks have not' (p. 14). When Rhoda is questioned by
Gertrude about Conjuror Trendle, she is suddenly
scared to think that Trendle might identify her as the
cause of Gertrude's strange affliction. The reader
empathises (see Literary Terms) with Rhoda; this
creates **suspense** (see Literary Terms) and a curiosity as
to how events will turn out.

The more educated upper classes did not share the faith
in witchcraft of the lower classes, and Thomas Hardy
draws upon this to emphasise the vanity and
desperation of Mrs Lodge. She initially consults doctors
in search of a cure and ridicules the people who have
suggested that a conjuror may help her: 'O, how could
my people be so superstitious as to recommend a man
of that sort!' (p. 14); the divide between the classes is
evident. She dismisses the idea until her desperation

*Compare
Gertrude's
obsession with a
cure to Rhoda's
earlier obsession
with Gertrude.*

drives her to seek any cure whatsoever. She, too, now
believes her disfigurement is a curse and that it is the
cause of the unhappiness in her marriage. The
magnitude of her vanity and her despair are emphasised
by her obsession with the gruesome suggested cure on
her second visit to Conjuror Trendle.

Thomas Hardy's use of an **omniscient narrator** (see
Literary Terms) allows him to draw a **parallel** (see
Literary Terms) between Gertrude and Rhoda through
the descriptions of their subconscious states of mind:
Gertrude's 'unconscious prayer' (p. 23) is for a person to
be hanged soon, whether they are guilty or innocent;
while in 'her secret heart' Rhoda 'did not altogether

object to a slight diminution of her successor's beauty'
(p. 13), though she does not wish upon Gertrude any
physical pain.

Parts VII and VIII of the story ('A Ride' and 'A Water-
side Hermit') concentrate on Gertrude's elaborate plans
to carry out the cure. These serve to build up the
tension by postponing the horrific act that Gertrude is
determined to commit. The reader is alerted by the
opportune absence of Farmer Lodge which allows
Gertrude to avoid explaining her whereabouts. As
Gertrude lays her hand on the hanged young man's
neck in the final section, the action of the story reaches
a **climax** (see Literary Terms). All the main characters
are together for the first time and Gertrude is castigated
by Rhoda. Rhoda's suffering – witnessing her innocent
son's hanging – throws into relief the vanity and
superficiality of Gertrude. The final paragraph brings
the story full circle as it ends with Rhoda returning to
her village and milking cows, and refusing to accept the
annuity which Farmer Lodge has bequeathed her.

Do you think the
characters get
what they
deserve?

GLOSSARY   **lorn** forlorn, forsaken
              supernumerary temporarily hired as extra workers
              tisty-tosty pretty, attractive
              barton farmyard
              'A (dialect) he
              laved washed in
              milchers (dialect) cows kept for milking
              yeoman a person who cultivates his own land
              riband ribbon, strip
              dilatoriness tendency to delay or waste time
              ricks stacks of hay or straw
              comely attractive
              gownd (dialect) gown
              incubus spectre or evil spirit
              chimmer (dialect) bedroom
              alluvial soil fertile soil deposited on a flood plain

Wessex King Ina, presented to after-ages as Lear in Shakespeare's *King Lear* the king suffers inner turmoil as he wanders on the heath

furze gorse

prosiness dullness

nostrums quack medicines

assize trial

fillip boost, stimulation

desuetude disuse

obdurate stubborn

taciturnity silence; unwillingness to talk

Enclosure Acts Acts of Parliament, passed with increasing frequency from 1760, which allowed tracts of common land to be enclosed by hedges

turbary privileges the right to dig peat for fuel on another's land

harum-skarum reckless, irresponsible

a-scram dialect term used to describe an ugly wound

wownd (dialect) wound

wicket small door

rencounter unexpected meeting

galvanism electrical current used to activate nerves or muscles

CHARACTERS

Rhoda

Rhoda Brook is portrayed as an isolated character who avoids the company of others. She is described as 'thin' and 'worn', suggesting she has suffered in the past. She has had a relationship with the local landowner and borne him a son – given the context of this story, she is evidently a strong character to have remained close to the community, if not as a part of it. She is conscious of the social divide between herself and Farmer Lodge, and this is shown in her speculative comments about his new wife.

Thomas Hardy draws the reader's attention to the impoverished lifestyle of Rhoda and her son, which establishes some **sympathy** (see Literary Terms) for her. The reader recognises Rhoda's satisfaction on discovering she is taller than Mrs Lodge, and also the small compensation this provides when comparing herself to a lady. She is curious about Farmer Lodge's wife, but carefully avoids meeting her.

Rhoda is presented as a passive victim.

She becomes preoccupied by her imagined picture of Mrs Lodge, and the reader begins to suspect she has hidden feelings about the situation. It seems Rhoda is the victim of the rigid social system of the time; she is also portrayed as the victim in her nightmare, in which she is cruelly taunted by Mrs Lodge. It is **ironic** (see Literary Terms) that she is visited the next day by the real Mrs Lodge. The **omniscient narrator** (see Literary Terms) informs us that she is in fact glad to have met Gertrude, and it is through Rhoda's eyes that she is described as an 'innocent young thing' who 'should have her blessing and not her curse' (p. 10).

Rhoda is presented as a prudent, pragmatic character who has passively accepted her rejection by Farmer Lodge and the harsh lifestyle which is the result of it. She is described as possessing 'the strength that endures' (p. 10). Although she is ostracised by the locals, she remains dignified, and disregards the fact that they think she is a witch – before the fateful nightmare and Mrs Lodge's mysterious injury, at least.

It is through concern for Gertrude's predicament that Rhoda agrees to visit Conjuror Trendle, against her better judgement. She is moved by the innocence and kindness of Gertrude, which indicates in Rhoda a genuine compassion, given her circumstances. As the gossip circulates that she is the cause of Gertrude's affliction, she is sympathetically portrayed by Thomas Hardy as the victim as 'her face grew sadder and

thinner' (p. 18) before she and her son leave
Holmstoke.

In the final part of the story Thomas Hardy again
sympathises with Rhoda and her situation. By
maintaining the anonymity of the hanged man,
Thomas Hardy gives greater impact to Rhoda's
discovery of Gertrude; her suffering is evident and she
is a pitiable character. When she returns to her
neighbourhood some time later, she gains dignity in her
refusal of the money left to her by the now deceased
Farmer Lodge. She disdains the company of others who
wonder 'what sombre thoughts were beating inside that
impassive, wrinkled brow' (p. 33).

Gertrude

It is the dairy workers who first mention Gertrude,
describing her as 'a rosy-cheeked, tisty-tosty little body'
(p. 1). They also draw our attention to her youthfulness
compared to Farmer Lodge. The description of
Gertrude on her way home with her new husband
completes the picture of a young, pretty woman who
has a cheerfully innocent perception of the world. She
is embarrassed by the staring of Rhoda's son and by the
general interest in her amongst the locals. Her shame at
the noise of her dress brushing against the pews on her
first visit to the local church also shows how she prefers
not to show her wealth ostentatiously.

Her ingenuous description to Rhoda of her mysterious
injury is the beginning of the disastrous chain of events
that forms the story. She confides in Rhoda and we
glimpse the emotional strain Gertrude is under as she
tells her of the effect on her marriage. Thomas Hardy
suggests that Gertrude has few pretensions other than
her vanity.

Preoccupation with appearance is central to Gertrude's
character and she becomes 'an irritable, superstitious
woman' (p. 19). The contrast between Gertrude and

Thomas Hardy contrasts Gertrude with Rhoda throughout the story.

Rhoda is evident. Gertrude is shown to be shallow and petty in allowing a superficial thing like her appearance have such a devastating effect on her life. Rhoda, however, has endured far greater hardship in life.

Gertrude's faith in herself dwindles, and her rational perspective on life is destroyed when put to the test. It is her obsession with looking beautiful that leads her to try a variety of discredited cures 'which in her schoolgirl time she would have ridiculed as folly' (p. 19). It seems age has brought only superficial wisdom to Gertrude. When she is told about 'the turn o' the blood' her obsession increases still further, as she wishes for someone to be hanged as soon as possible – Gertrude is shown to be persistently vain and selfish.

Gertrude becomes obsessed with the search for a cure.

It is **ironic** (see Literary Terms) that Gertrude is shown to most rational and practical when she is planning to attend the hanging. She remains resolute about carrying out the cure, despite its gruesome nature. The cure is effective but Gertrude is destroyed by the discovery that the hanged youth is the son of Rhoda and Farmer Lodge. The description of the discovery forces the reader to consider Gertrude's vanity and superficiality: her actions show no compassion or caring for anyone other than herself.

The **narrator** (see Literary Terms) describes Gertrude's death as having been caused by 'the severe strain, physical and mental, to which she had subjected herself during the previous twenty-four hours' (p. 32). She is clearly the victim of her own vanity, and her 'delicate vitality' is shown to be inadequate for survival in what Thomas Hardy presents as a harsh and unforgiving world.

Farmer Lodge

Thomas Hardy presents Farmer Lodge as an attractive, though aging man. He is described in terms that emphasise his affluence and his vanity: 'he seemed pleased, and his waistcoat stuck out, and his great golden seals hung like a lord's' (p. 7). He is clearly satisfied that he has married such a young and beautiful woman – she is a more 'appropriate' wife than Rhoda Brook would have been (see Context & Setting on social class and conventions).

His character becomes less attractive as we learn that he has ignored his son and the poverty in which he and Rhoda live. Farmer Lodge has chosen to concede to the rules of a society which would not have tolerated him acknowledging his son or Rhoda after their relationship ended.

Like Gertrude, he places undue value upon appearances and we are told that she was 'the woman whom he had wooed for her grace and beauty' (p. 19). His reaction to her disfigurement exacerbates the situation, feeding Gertrude's obsession with her appearance. He wonders whether he is being punished by God for his selfish behaviour concerning Rhoda and her son.

Farmer Lodge's change has come too late.

After the death of his son and Gertrude, we learn that 'he eventually changed for the better, and appeared as a chastened and thoughtful man' (p. 32). But his selfish behaviour and superficial values have been seen to lead to disastrous consequences.

A *Identify the speaker.*

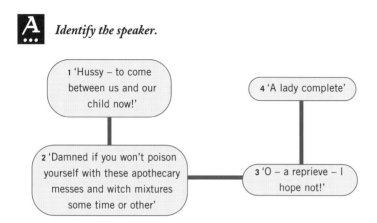

1 'Hussy – to come between us and our child now!'

4 'A lady complete'

2 'Damned if you won't poison yourself with these apothecary messes and witch mixtures some time or other'

3 'O – a reprieve – I hope not!'

Identify the person 'to whom' this comment refers.

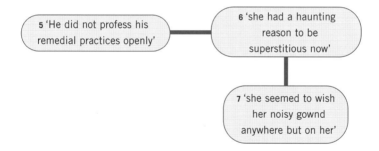

5 'He did not profess his remedial practices openly'

6 'she had a haunting reason to be superstitious now'

7 'she seemed to wish her noisy gownd anywhere but on her'

Check your answers on page 89.

B *Consider these issues.*

a The role played by superstition in the story. Does modern society hold similarly strong superstitions?

b How the description of Gertrude's plans creates **suspense** (see Literary Terms).

c How status within the community affects the actions of the characters.

d How the descriptions of the characters' physical appearances add to our understanding of them.

The Son's Veto

Detailed Summary

I   Thomas Hardy begins this short story with an intriguing description of Sophy Twycott's intricate hairstyle. She is in her wheelchair listening with her son to a band playing in a local park in suburban London. She is the object of much curiosity due to her disability and her hairstyle.

On their way home Randolph, her son, harshly corrects her speech, which he regards as inappropriate since she is now socially removed from people who use a regional dialect. Sophy accepts his chastisement and thinks about how events in her life have resulted in her present situation.

As a young woman living in a North Wessex village, she worked as a parlour-maid for the local parson, Mr Twycott, and his first wife, who died when Sophy was nineteen. Sam Hobson, a local gardener, wished to marry Sophy and she mentioned this to Mr Twycott. She and Sam quarrelled and called off the wedding, however, and Mr Twycott began himself to think of Sophy affectionately. He became ill and Sophy looked after him. Having taken him his meal on one occasion, she fell down the stairs, and was subsequently informed she must never walk again. The fact that she was caring for him when she fell endeared her to Mr Twycott, and he proposed to her. They married, and then moved to London, where people would not know that they were not from the same social class (see Context & Setting).

II   On the death of her husband Sophy is left with a personal income and a house he had bought for her to live in when he died. Her son attends a public school and the gulf between mother and son widens. She leads an uneventful life and she dreams about the village where she lived before her marriage. She enjoys watching the country people bringing produce to sell at Covent Garden market, and one day recognises Sam Hobson as one of the traders. They renew their acquaintance and she confides in Sam that she longs to live in the village where they grew up.

III   Sam persuades Sophy to travel with him on his way to Covent Garden one morning. Sophy realises that this would not be appropriate behaviour for someone of her social standing, but she is tempted by adventure. On the second journey with Sam he proposes to her, suggesting they return to North Wessex to set up a greengrocer's shop. She refuses to marry him because of the embarrassment it would cause her son if she were to marry someone of a lower social class. She decides to tell Randolph that she intends to marry Sam at some time in the future when it will not affect her son's life.

Randolph continually refuses to accept the idea of the marriage, and after many years of her pleading with him, he finally makes her swear that she will not marry Sam without his consent.

Sophy dies wishing Randolph would relent, and she is buried in her old village. Randolph, now a priest, accompanies her coffin, which passes Sam's shop on the way to the churchyard. Randolph resents the respectful presence of Sam outside his shop.

COMMENT   *The Son's Veto* is a vehicle for some of Thomas Hardy's most hostile comments on the divisive class system of the nineteenth century. The **tone** of the story is **didactic** (see Literary Terms) and condemnatory as Thomas Hardy criticises a class system that forces people to behave contrary to their instinctive desires (see also Context & Setting).

This style is also used in The Withered Arm.   In this story Thomas Hardy writes as an **omniscient narrator** (see Literary Terms), a technique which allows him to express the innermost thoughts of the characters, whilst also allowing him to comment on the characters and their situations and actions. In the first paragraph he describes Sophy's hairstyle in terms which suggest the futility of her life. She is then described as 'poor thing': Sophy is a pitiable character who also appears to be powerless.

At the beginning of the story the narrator is distanced from the characters and describes them as though he is also part of the gathering listening to the band, revealing details about Sophy's appearance in the way a curious bystander would discover them. The effect of this description creates an interest in the characters and a feeling of **suspense** (see Literary Terms) as we are told she is a woman with 'a story of some sort or other' (p. 35).

We overhear the conversation between mother and son as they return home. Sophy comments affectionately about the condition of her sick husband, using her regional dialect (see Language & Style). She is reprimanded by her son who insists she should use what is nowadays known as 'Standard English': the appropriate way for people of their social class to speak. We are immediately aware of the difference in class of the public schoolboy and his mother, and of how their relationship is dominated by him. In deference to her son, Sophy is silent for the rest of their journey. The son is presented as an irascible character and there is a sense of foreboding about the way he behaves towards his mother.

The **narrator** (see Literary Terms) recounts the events that have led to Sophy's current situation in **flashback** (see Literary Terms). Sophy is described as a young woman, working as a parlour-maid at the local vicarage. She is shown to be thoughtful and modest in the conversation she has with Sam, her admirer. The vicar is forced to consider reducing his staff after the death of his wife, and it is whilst considering this that he realises that Sophy is the person to whom he feels closest, since she is always present at the house; given his circumstances, the reader has some sympathy for him. The distance between them socially is emphasised in the description of Sophy's reaction to his proposal: 'she hardly dared refuse a personage so reverend and august in her eyes' (p. 39).

The narrator states that, in following his instinctive desires and marrying Sophy, Mr Twycott had knowingly 'committed social suicide'. The consequences of his actions are illustrated through the descriptions of the home they must abandon and their new home in London. Thomas Hardy suggests that the move away from their home town is necessary due to the inevitable social disapproval of their marriage, although he is evidently sympathetic to their having married despite this.

Thomas Hardy continues his criticism of the class system and its associated prejudice through his description of Sophy's married life. She is regarded with contempt because she occasionally uses a regional dialect, and she has few friends. She is made to feel inferior by her own son. The distress caused by her feelings of inadequacy is presented as disproportionate to the significance attached by society to appropriate behaviour. Life has treated Sophy harshly – she is no adversary for such an unforgiving and snobbish society, and is steadily destroyed by it.

Thomas Hardy describes Sophy at her happiest when she renews her friendship with Sam. There are many references to how inappropriate her behaviour is, although the reader sympathises with Sophy and is likely to be critical of the destructive nature of society. After her first trip to Covent Garden market, for example, the narrator comments: 'A woman of pure instincts, she knew there had been nothing really wrong in the journey, but supposed it conventionally to be very wrong indeed' (p. 46). Thomas Hardy presents natural human instincts and 'proper' behaviour as being in constant opposition. In making Sophy the defenceless victim of such prejudice, Thomas Hardy's criticism of class distinctions and divides is relentless.

Thomas Hardy is fiercely critical of the upper classes and he conveys this through the character of Randolph, Sophy's son. Randolph is one of Thomas Hardy's most abhorrent characters, presented as shallow and superficial, selecting the company of those who are affluent and who have high social status, and arrogantly disregarding people of lower classes – even his own mother. His treatment of Sophy is cruel in the extreme, and it is implied that his actions are necessary in order for him to maintain his position in society.

There is a build-up of **suspense** (see Literary Terms) as Sophy tries again and again to persuade Randolph to allow her to marry Sam. The **climax** (see Literary Terms) of the story is when Randolph forces his mother to swear that she will not marry without his permission. The **objective** description of her funeral in the final paragraph increases the **pathos** of her death and the sense of **closure** (see Literary Terms). Sophy sacrifices her happiness, and hence her life, in order that her son may not be socially damaged by her marriage to Sam.

GLOSSARY   **poll** part of the head where the hair grows
flexuous full-figured
milieu immediate environment
appertained belonged
Parleyings discussions, pleas

CHARACTERS

Sophy

The opening description of Sophy's hairstyle seemingly praises her skill and achievement in creating such a work of art. By contrast, however, the next paragraph serves to present her as a pitiable character whose life is futile and dreary. Her confinement to a wheelchair is **symbolic** (see Literary Terms) of her lack of power and her dominance by other characters.

Thomas Hardy presents Sophy in a sympathetic way, emphasising her innocence and loyalty when he describes the circumstances which lead to her marrying Mr Twycott. She is a humble character whose actions are influenced by her wish to please others, rather than to satisfy her own desires. Thomas Hardy establishes this early in the story, as it is a characteristic that will have disastrous consequences later.

Once Sophy is removed from her familiar surroundings and social equals she becomes even more pitiable. She is the victim of social snobbery, and despite her efforts to improve herself socially, she remains at heart a lower-class character: 'her husband had taken much trouble with her education; but she still held confused ideas on the use of "was" and "were", which did not beget a

What do the changes in Sophy's tastes after Mr Twycott's death indicate about their relationship?

respect for her among the few acquaintances she made' (p. 40). When her husband dies we are told 'she soon lost the little artificial tastes she had acquired from him' (p. 42), while her son becomes less tolerant of her social failings.

Thomas Hardy directs the reader to judge Sophy favourably. Her social inadequacies are put into perspective by her love for and loyalty to her son: 'As yet he was far from being man enough – if he ever would be – to rate these sins of hers at their true infinitesimal value beside the yearning fondness that welled up and remained penned in her heart' (p. 42). It is clear that Thomas Hardy values compassion and love more highly than social acceptability, and he is critical of those who do not share these values.

Randolph

To the detached observer at the beginning of the story, Randolph is a disagreeable character. He corrects his mother's speech 'with an impatient fastidiousness that was almost harsh' (p. 36). Initially this could be viewed as a petulant outburst since he is young, but his intolerance of his mother and her lower-class origins increases as he becomes older and more educated. By the end of the story we are told that his education 'had by this time sufficiently ousted his humanity'. Randolph embodies many of the unappealing prejudices held by society at the time and he is a means by which Thomas Hardy can express his own loathing of such a destructive and divisive class system.

Consider Randolph's behaviour at the cricket match.

Randolph dominates his mother's life. She adores him and recognises her inadequacies; he finds her insufferable and is increasingly irritated and embarrassed by her social failings. He regards her as 'a mother whose mistakes and origin it was his painful lot as a gentleman to blush for' (p. 42). Randolph's treatment of his mother is cruel and inhumane: he forces her to sacrifice potential happiness so that his own place in society will not be threatened. It is **ironic** (see Literary Terms) that a character so lacking in compassion becomes a priest.

Sam Hobson   Thomas Hardy presents Sam as an honest and loyal character. He respects Sophy's changed circumstances but recognises she is lonely and unhappy in her new society. It is in this uneducated and lower-class grocer that we recognise qualities and virtues that we find admirable. His mourning of Sophy at the end of the story increases the **pathos** (see Literary Terms) of the ending.

Mr Twycott   The vicar of Gaymead serves to illustrate the serious consequences of acting on human desires rather than behaving appropriately according to the conventions of society. In his loneliness after the death of his wife, he finds the tenderness in Sophy endearing. On marrying Sophy, his social inferior, he is aware of their unacceptability as a couple, and they move to the relative anonymity of London to avoid being ostracised.

Compare Mr Twycott's treatment of Sophy to her treatment by Randolph.   Mr Twycott's compassion is illustrated by his attempts to 'educate' Sophy in the ways of upper-class society: 'She showed a natural aptitude for little domestic refinements, so far as related to things and manners; but in what is called culture she was less intuitive' (p. 40). He makes provisions for her after his death, thereby allowing her some independence. He recognises her inadequacies and makes allowances for them.

A *Identify the speaker.*

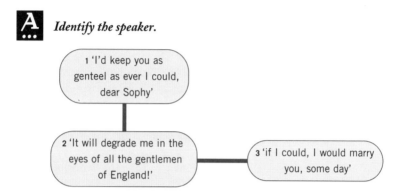

1 'I'd keep you as genteel as ever I could, dear Sophy'

2 'It will degrade me in the eyes of all the gentlemen of England!'

3 'if I could, I would marry you, some day'

Identify the person(s) 'to whom' this comment refers.

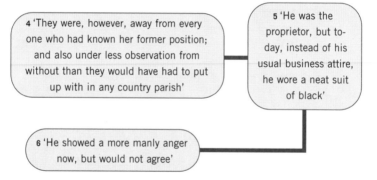

4 'They were, however, away from every one who had known her former position; and also under less observation from without than they would have had to put up with in any country parish'

5 'He was the proprietor, but to-day, instead of his usual business attire, he wore a neat suit of black'

6 'He showed a more manly anger now, but would not agree'

Check your answers on page 89.

B *Consider these issues.*

a The justification for Randolph's actions.

b Mr Twycott's motivation for marrying Sophy, even though he knows it to be 'social suicide'.

c Whether such a story could be set in modern times.

d The implications of Randolph becoming a member of the clergy.

DETAILED SUMMARY

The story begins with a description of Tony Kytes. His face is slightly scarred by smallpox, but not enough to prevent women finding him rather attractive. We are told that 'in return for their likings he loved 'em in shoals.' We also learn of his supposed engagement to Milly Richards.

Driving his father's waggon home from market one day, Tony meets one of his former sweethearts, Unity Sallet. She asks him for a lift home and he cannot refuse. Unity starts flirting with Tony, who is obviously flattered. He then sees Milly Richards in the distance and is aware of the compromising situation he is in. To avoid having to explain himself to Milly, he asks Unity to hide under the tarpaulin in the waggon. He tries to avoid giving Milly a ride home, but cannot refuse her.

As they ride on, Tony sees another former sweetheart, Hannah Jolliver, in the distance. He uses flattery to persuade Milly to hide under some sacks in the waggon so that it will appear he is alone when he meets Hannah. Hannah demands to ride with Tony and once the waggon sets off again their conversation becomes flirtatious. Tony denies being engaged to Milly and suggests to Hannah that he would rather marry her. Milly, still under the sacks, overhears this and cries out. Tony tries to change the subject, worried that Hannah will find out that Milly and Unity are hiding in the waggon.

Tony's father, in a nearby field, sees him riding with Hannah, knowing he is engaged to Milly. Glad to have an excuse to stop the conversation, Tony goes to speak to his father, leaving Hannah in control of the horse and waggon. Tony's father is concerned about the scandal there would be if anyone else were to see his son riding with another woman. Tony explains his current predicament, and his father advises him to marry Milly. His father's advice makes Tony think that he should definitely not marry Milly.

Whilst Tony is talking to his father, Hannah loses control of the horse, causing Milly to discover that Unity is also hiding in the waggon. They crash and the three women are thrown into the road.

Tony tries to calm the women by declaring that he and Hannah are going to be married. However, Hannah's father appears and advises his daughter not to marry Tony. She turns down Tony's offer of marriage. Tony then asks Unity to be his wife; she also declines. Finally he asks Milly to marry him and she accepts. They are married shortly after.

COMMENT

Compare the tone of this story to that of Absent-mindedness in a Parish Choir.

The title of this short story creates expectations of a character who is harsh and malicious in his deceptions. However, this is immediately undermined by the description of the humorous Tony Kytes in the first paragraph. The **first-person narrative** style of this short story establishes an informal, friendly **tone** (see Literary Terms). The narrator speaks with a dialect which creates the sense of an amusing **anecdote** (see Literary Terms) shared between friends, and this anecdotal style allows for some embellishment of events by the

narrator. The narrator is bemused by the behaviour of
the characters, and he recounts the story in a way which
invites the reader to view their behaviour as ridiculous
too.

The initial description of Tony Kytes also serves to
establish the theme of relationships between men and
women, and to highlight the fact that there is no
rational means to account for being found attractive:
''Twas a little, round, firm, tight face, with a seam here
and there left by the smallpox, but not enough to hurt
his looks in a woman's eye.'

The action of the story is confined to one short journey,
and therefore the **plot** (see Literary Terms) moves
swiftly. The situation quickly becomes irretrievable for
Tony and the **suspense** (see Literary Terms) builds as
he hides first one and then another sweetheart in his
waggon. Tony's meeting with his father serves to delay
the inevitable discovery of his deception which
constitutes the **climax** (see Literary Terms) of the story.
Events become more and more ridiculous, and we learn
that even after their humiliating treatment by Tony, all
three women would still have married him. Only Milly
accepts his proposal, however, the other two preferring
to salvage some dignity from the situation.

In this story Thomas Hardy takes a wry look at
relationships between men and women. His choice of a
first-person narrator (see Literary Terms) allows the
story to remain amusing, despite the humiliation at the
end. The narrator refrains from criticising any of the
characters' behaviour, instead recounting the tale as an
example of the apparently incomprehensible way in
which men and women behave towards each other. The
'rare party' thrown to celebrate the wedding of Tony
and Milly provides a sense of **closure** (see Literary
Terms), and reinforces the view that Tony's deceptions
were more laughable than harmful.

GLOSSARY   **seam** (dialect) scar

banns public notification of the intention to marry

nunny-watch (dialect) predicament

miff (dialect) argument or fuss

swound (dialect) faint or swoon

rare exceptionally good

CHARACTERS

Tony Kytes

Thomas Hardy introduces Tony Kytes as an enviable character in the eyes of the **narrator** (see Literary Terms). Tony's attractiveness to women is unaccountable, and it is, from the narrator's point of view, only natural for him to take advantage of this. Indeed, throughout the story, Tony's inability to deny his affection for Unity and Hannah is exacerbated by their behaviour towards him.

The 'arch-deceiver' expected from the title is continually undermined as the story unfolds. Tony's feeble excuses to persuade Unity and Milly to hide in the waggon suggest opportunist rather than premeditated actions. His attempts to convince Hannah that she is the one he wishes to marry are humorously described, since the reader is aware that Milly can hear their conversation: he speaks to Hannah 'in a whisper', and when she questions his quiet tone of voice he claims he has 'a kind of hoarseness'.

Tony finally decides to ask Hannah to marry him, a decision arrived at because 'of all things that could have happened to wean him from Milly there was nothing so powerful as his father's recommending her' (p. 58). Tony's complete lack of respect for women is evident, and their behaviour does not demand respect. His wish to pacify them at the end suggests his complete incomprehension of the humiliation he has caused them to suffer. He cannot

Look carefully at the way in which the two women turn down Tony's offer of marriage.

understand why both Hannah and Unity turn down his offer of marriage, but his faith in the way women behave remains unshaken as he finally persuades Milly that 'it do seem as if fate had ordained that it should be you and I, or nobody.'

At the end of the story Tony appears to be unaffected by recent events. He is presented as a pragmatic character who finally marries his original choice of bride, evidently the more attractive alternative to nobody. The hasty putting-up of the banns 'the very next Sunday' could imply a new-found resoluteness, or a wish to avoid the risk of any further wavering on Tony's part. Either way, the couple are seen publicly to be happy.

Milly Richards

Milly is the only character in this short story to elicit any **sympathy** from the **narrator** (see Literary Terms), and hence from the reader. She is described in admirable, though relatively unexciting, terms as 'a nice, light, small, tender little thing' (p. 51). When she meets Tony she pouts and playfully tells him off for being late. She is presented as a gullible character, one who is easily persuaded by promises of marriage to hide in the waggon.

Her heartfelt moan on hearing Tony declare his love for Hannah adds **pathos** (see Literary Terms) to the comical situation. She attempts to regain some dignity from the situation when she discovers Unity under the tarpaulin – 'Well, if this isn't disgraceful!' (p. 58) – and accuses Unity of improper behaviour with an engaged man. The subsequent confrontation between the three women and Tony only increases her humiliation, however. In light of this humiliation we may find her decision to accept Tony as her husband ill-judged; on the other hand, we may see her choice as pragmatic and sensible, since the ending of the story reinforces the

Do you think Milly is right to marry Tony?

view that the whole incident was of little significance in the long run.

Hannah
Jolliver and
Unity Sallet

Tony's father recommends that Tony should marry 'Whichever of 'em did *not* ask to ride with thee' (p. 57). The implication of this advice is that in the long run Tony will appreciate a wife who is less domineering, manipulative and vain than Hannah and Unity are. Each flirts with Tony and teases him with the fact that she is the more suitable wife for him.

Their vanity is confirmed at the end of the story when they both turn down Tony's offer of marriage. Hannah is described as being in a 'tantrum' because of the scratch from a bramble on her face. She refuses Tony's offer of marriage, but she is 'thinking and hoping he would ask her again'. Unity is more vehement in her refusal of Tony, although when she walks away she looks back 'to see if he was following her'.

A *Identify the speaker.*

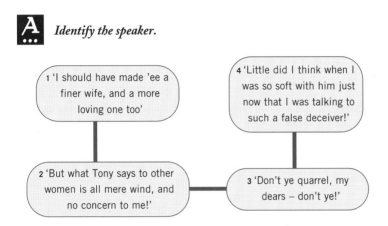

1 'I should have made 'ee a finer wife, and a more loving one too'

4 'Little did I think when I was so soft with him just now that I was talking to such a false deceiver!'

2 'But what Tony says to other women is all mere wind, and no concern to me!'

3 'Don't ye quarrel, my dears – don't ye!'

Identify the person 'to whom' this comment refers.

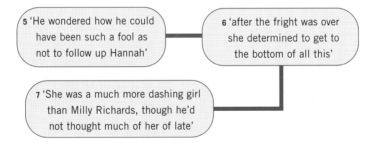

5 'He wondered how he could have been such a fool as not to follow up Hannah'

6 'after the fright was over she determined to get to the bottom of all this'

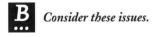

7 'She was a much more dashing girl than Milly Richards, though he'd not thought much of her of late'

Check your answers on page 89.

B *Consider these issues.*

a The effect of the humorous **tone** of the **narrative** (see Literary Terms).

b To what extent you think the characters behave appropriately.

c What Thomas Hardy's views on marriage might have been.

d The effect which a more formal **narrator** (see Literary Terms) would have on the story.

ABSENT-MINDEDNESS IN A PARISH CHOIR

A local band of musicians has been playing at various venues throughout the busy Christmas season. They are due to play in the local church one cold afternoon, and one of the band members has brought along some hot brandy and beer to keep them warm. They drink the alcohol during the church service and fall asleep during the sermon.

In the darkness of the musicians' gallery, they are suddenly woken when they are required to play. They completely forget where they are, and instead of playing the hymn they play a raunchy song, one that they had been playing at all the parties. The parson, the squire and visiting gentry are present in the church and are appalled by the tune, and outraged that it should be played in a church.

The musicians are repentant, but they are not forgiven. The next week the squire buys a barrel-organ which plays hymns mechanically, and so dispenses with the musicians forever.

COMMENT   This short story is written using a **first-person narrator**, giving the story an amusing **anecdotal** (see

Literary Terms) style similar to that of *Tony Kytes, the Arch-Deceiver*. Thomas Hardy creates a sense of intrigue in the first few sentences as we learn that it was 'the last Sunday ever they played in Longpuddle church gallery'. A familiarity with the musicians is evident as they are all introduced by their names and their instruments.

The offence caused by the musicians is not deliberate.

The narrator moves swiftly to the 'fatal day'. The musicians see no wrong in consuming the alcohol in the church, and it is clear that no offence or malice was intended – the alcohol was to make them feel 'quite comfortable and warm'. A busy schedule and the influence of the alcohol conspire to cause the musicians to forget their surroundings and play an inappropriate tune in church. Thomas Hardy illustrates the division of the upper and lower classes by adding that the tune they played was 'the favourite jig of our neighbourhood at that time'. The lower classes enjoyed dances and tunes which the upper classes would have regarded as improper and unholy.

The humour of the situation is emphasised as the musicians play so loudly that at first they cannot hear the congregation's outburst. This contrasts with the outrage of the parson and the squire, which is shown to be excessive and unjustified. Thomas Hardy draws attention to the hypocrisy of the squire: 'a wickedish man' who on this occasion 'happened to be on the Lord's side' because there are important visitors present. It is ultimately the squire who will not forgive the musicians and who replaces them with the barrel-organ. The end of the story highlights the lack of human warmth and tolerance shown by the upper classes and the church. Decorum is restored by employing 'a really respectable man to turn the winch' of the barrel-organ.

GLOSSARY   **gallery** balcony

serpent an old-fashioned wind instrument having the shape of a snake

reels lively communal dances

Absolution the remission of sin pronounced by the priest in the Christian sacrament of penance

Creed the Apostles' Creed, a concise statement of belief in the essential Christian doctrines

Sodom and Gomorrah Old Testament cities destroyed by God as punishment for their inhabitants' vice and depravity

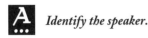

A *Identify the speaker.*

1 'Please the Lord I won't stand this numbing weather no longer: this afternoon we'll have something in our insides to make us warm, if it cost a king's ransom'

2 'What! In this reverent edifice! What!'

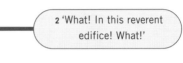

Identify the person(s) 'to whom' this comment refers.

3 'That very week he sent for a barrel-organ that would play two-and-twenty new psalm-tunes, so exact and particular that, however sinful inclined you was, you could play nothing but psalm-tunes whatsomever'

4 'as the sermon went on – most unfortunately for 'em it was a long one that afternoon – they fell asleep, every man jack of 'em; and there they slept on as sound as rocks'

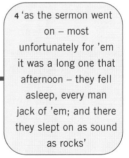

Check your answers on page 89.

B *Consider these issues.*

a How the division between the upper and lower classes is illustrated by this story.

b How the squire's attitude contrasts with the Christian ideal of forgiveness.

c The implications of replacing the musicians with the barrel-organ.

d How the characters' behaviour is influenced by their status.

DETAILED SUMMARY

I   The **narrator** (see Literary Terms) describes the downs of the rural South-West of England, and considers how they must have looked ninety years previously, when the events about to be recounted took place. He explains that the story was told to him by Phyllis Grove when he was fifteen and she was an elderly woman. The story proper then begins.

It is the time of the Napoleonic Wars. Phyllis and her father, a former doctor, live in an isolated hamlet and despite this, Phyllis has become engaged to a respectable, if rather average, gentleman called Humphrey Gould. Shortly after becoming engaged, he leaves the area and goes to Bath, promising to return soon. Whilst he is away, the 'celebrated' York Hussars and other regiments of the King's soldiers set up camp close to the hamlet.

II   Phyllis is intrigued by the York Hussars, and she notices one soldier in particular who looks very sad. She feels sorry for him and they become friends. Phyllis pities him being away from his home in Germany and the people he loves. She refrains from becoming more than friends, however, because she is still engaged to Humphrey Gould.

III   The gossip in Bath that Humphrey does not consider himself engaged to Phyllis reaches her through a friend of her father. Phyllis is not upset by this news, and she becomes more friendly with Matthäus Tina, the lonely Hussar. Their relationship develops into a romance.

Matthäus reveals his hatred for the Hussars and his homesickness. He plans to run away from the legion, but he realises that he would not be able to marry Phyllis. She agrees that her father would not allow her to marry a disgraced soldier beneath her own social standing.

Phyllis's father confronts her about her liaison with Matthäus. He believes her actions to be outrageous and declares that he is planning to send her to stay with her aunt, to avoid any further scandal. Phyllis determines to run away with Matthäus and his friend Christoph, who also wishes to desert.

IV   The evening of the escape arrives and Phyllis waits for the arrival of Matthäus in a concealed place on the highway. Whilst she is waiting there Humphrey Gould arrives with a friend and she overhears him admitting how badly he has treated her. He has brought her a present as a 'peace-offering'. On hearing this, Phyllis realises the serious consequences her planned flight will have. She decides not to run away with her beloved Matthäus, but to remain loyal to her promise to marry Humphrey. When Matthäus arrives, she remains resolved to stay, despite his pleading.

The next morning she finds that Humphrey has already called to see her. He has left her a gift: a mirror in a silver frame. She feels bound to honour her former promise of marriage and prepares to meet him.

V   Phyllis and Humphrey go for a walk, during which he tells her he is married. The gift of the mirror was intended to persuade her to declare publicly that she could not marry him, thereby preventing a scandal and embarrassing him.

Phyllis is in a state of shock for several days. She remains at home pining for Matthäus. When she does finally venture outdoors one day, she goes to the place where she used to meet him. From there she can see the army camp. She gradually realises that the Hussars are making preparations for an execution by firing-squad. She is horrified when she realises the Hussars to be executed are Matthäus and Christoph.

Transfixed, Phyllis watches their execution. A few moments later she is discovered unconscious by her father.

Phyllis tends the graves of the two Hussars and is buried close to them when she dies.

COMMENT

Contrast the tone of this story with that of Tony Kytes, the Arch-Deceiver and Absent-mindedness in a Parish Choir.

In this short story, the **narrator** (see Literary Terms) claims to be relating the story as it was told to him by Phyllis herself. This creates **sympathy** for Phyllis, and it allows Thomas Hardy to create a more poignant **tone** (see Literary Terms) through the detached perspective of the narrator. The title itself establishes expectations of a sad and poignant story.

A vivid sense of place is established at the beginning of the story, romantically evoking past times when the Hussars were camped there. The narrator imagines he can still hear 'the old trumpet and bugle calls', and recalls times when soldiers were 'monumental objects'. The isolation of the place is emphasised, as is the impact of the visiting soldiers.

Thomas Hardy explores the theme of social injustice in this short story through the engagement of Phyllis Grove to Humphrey Gould. Marriages between classes were frowned upon by the upper classes (see Context &

Setting), and the engagement is seen to be a triumph for Phyllis. Humphrey, however, is presented as a mercenary and heartless character for whom marriage is a means of social improvement – although he is of a higher class than Phyllis, he is 'as poor as a crow' (p. 68). In this short story he embodies the prejudices of the upper classes, and their disregard for anyone of a lower class.

Phyllis's trust in Humphrey is betrayed.

The tenacity Phyllis displays in waiting for Humphrey to return and honour his promise is cruelly repaid by his deception. She is perceived to behave honourably throughout the story, repressing her own feelings for Matthäus until she believes Humphrey to have abandoned the engagement. This contrasts with the deliberate and status-motivated actions of Humphrey Gould. The power of the unwritten rules of society at that time are highlighted when Phyllis is almost prepared to abandon her escape because of the scandal it would cause.

Matthäus's behaviour towards Phyllis is exemplary, and his situation, shared with the other German soldiers, is presented so as to demand the reader's sympathy: 'Their bodies were here, but their hearts and minds were always far away in their dear fatherland, of which – brave men and stoical as they were in many ways – they would speak with tears in their eyes' (p. 71). The execution at the end of the story highlights the brutality of the army and raises the question of the kind of behaviour that is appropriate in a civilised society.

The ending of the story is told **objectively** (see Literary Terms), and this increases its poignancy. The impersonal entries in the register of burials reinforce the overwhelming harshness of the deserters' execution. The ending is given more impact by the immediacy of bringing the events into the present day. The brevity of the last sentence adds a sense of finality and hopelessness, whilst reiterating Phyllis's continued affection for Matthäus.

GLOSSARY   **midden-heaps** rubbish heaps

impedimenta travelling equipment

the watering-place *bourgeoisie* the affluent and fashionable middle classes of the neighbouring spa town

Desdemona like Desdemona in Shakespeare's *Othello*, Phyllis is attracted to a foreigner who seems to have an exciting and exotic background

appurtenances less significant attributes

meine Liebliche (German) my darling

the courage which at the critical instant failed Cleopatra of Egypt a reference to the moment in Shakespeare's *Antony and Cleopatra* when Cleopatra leads her ships away from battle with Caesar

as dead as the camp of the Assyrians after the passage of the Destroying Angel a reference to the biblical story in which the Angel of Death descends upon Egypt, killing everyone who does not have the blood of a sacrificed lamb painted above the entrance to their dwelling

repoussé decorated in relief

tippet cape covering the shoulders

propitiate appease

carbines light rifles

CHARACTERS

Phyllis Grove   The isolated location of the village in which Phyllis lives makes her 'so shy that if she met a stranger anywhere in her short rambles she felt ashamed at his gaze, walked awkwardly, and blushed to her shoulders' (p. 67). She is inexperienced in relationships and her naïveté is reflected in her actions throughout the story. There is no mention of her mother, and it seems that she has no model on which to base her behaviour other

than the accepted code of conduct of the time. This makes her vulnerable to both the false promises of Humphrey Gould and the romantic promises of Matthäus Tina.

Phyllis is childlike in her fascination with the Hussars' camp, and watches it from the top of her garden wall. The acquaintance with Matthäus develops as 'she pitied him, and learnt his history' (p. 71). She behaves appropriately, considering herself engaged to Humphrey, until she hears that he does not consider himself formally engaged to her. Her inexperience of relationships is emphasised in her view of Matthäus as 'almost an ideal being' and 'the subject of a fascinating dream' (p. 73). She is attracted to a romantic notion of Matthäus, a notion to which his sad stories contribute.

When Matthäus suggests they marry, Phyllis is brought back to reality, and her concerns reflect the conventional views of the time. In practical terms she cannot really consider marrying him. She is uncomfortable with his romantic plan for them to run away to Germany – for a young woman brought up in such isolation this 'vague' and 'venturesome' plan would be a frightening prospect. However, circumstances conspire to cause Phyllis to change her mind, as her father provides the incentive to agree to Matthäus's proposal.

Thomas Hardy creates **sympathy** (see Literary Terms) for Phyllis through the unfortunate sequence of events. When she discovers Humphrey has returned she assumes from what she overhears that he intends to marry her. She decides to conform to the conventions of society and marry him, abandoning any hope of happiness. Humphrey has in fact returned to beg her to break off their engagement since he is already married. Once Phyllis realises this she becomes depressed. She is described as 'melancholy' (p. 83) and spends her time regretting not leaving with Matthäus and dreaming about their meetings. The execution is described in a detached manner, and the impact of the revelation that it is Matthäus and his friend mirrors the horror felt by Phyllis. Little detail is given about her life after these events except that she is buried close to the two soldiers in later years.

Humphrey
Gould

Humphrey Gould appears very little in the story but he has a substantial impact on the **plot** (see Literary Terms). He is described in bland terms as 'neither good-looking nor positively plain' (p. 67), but he is one of the 'idlers' who move about the country following the fashionable Royal Court. The fact that he has no money and yet maintains this fashionable lifestyle creates suspicion about his motives for wanting to marry Phyllis. His departure for Bath and his continued excuses for not returning increase this suspicion.

Compare
Humphrey with
the other upper-
class characters in
this collection of
short stories.

The conversation which Phyllis overhears when waiting for Matthäus is open to misinterpretation, perhaps forcing the reader at this point to reassess Humphrey, just as Phyllis does. This adds to the **suspense** (see Literary Terms) surrounding their eventual meeting. Humphrey's confession to Phyllis and his plea for her help are petty in contrast to the confusion in Phyllis's life. Through the character of Humphrey Gould, Thomas Hardy is criticising the lack of morals of the upper classes (see also Themes on Moral Standards).

Matthäus
Tina

Matthäus Tina is the 'Melancholy Hussar' of the title. He is presented as a romantic figure with passionate feelings. He allows his feelings to govern his decisions in life – in this respect he contrasts with the other characters, who are governed by concerns about how their behaviour will be viewed by society. His passionate nature unsettles Phyllis, and it is evident that such impulsiveness will not be tolerated by the military, as on one occasion he is demoted after returning late to the camp.

Matthäus's behaviour towards Phyllis is honourable – he is 'virtuous and kind' (p. 77) – but his scheme for escaping from England 'almost appalled her' (p. 76). He does not urge Phyllis to leave with him when she tells him she has changed her mind. His ignominious death is shocking: Thomas Hardy is showing how society does not tolerate dissent or non-conformity.

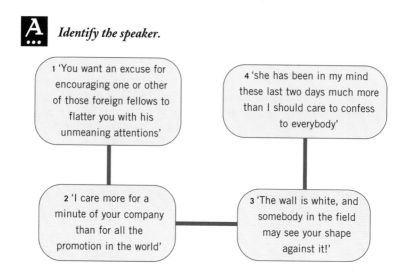

A *Identify the speaker.*

1 'You want an excuse for encouraging one or other of those foreign fellows to flatter you with his unmeaning attentions'

4 'she has been in my mind these last two days much more than I should care to confess to everybody'

2 'I care more for a minute of your company than for all the promotion in the world'

3 'The wall is white, and somebody in the field may see your shape against it!'

Identify the person 'to whom' this comment refers.

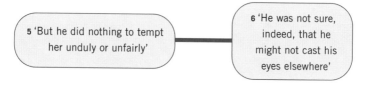

5 'But he did nothing to tempt her unduly or unfairly'

6 'He was not sure, indeed, that he might not cast his eyes elsewhere'

Check your answers on page 89.

B *Consider these issues.*

a The effect social acceptability has upon the way the characters behave.

b The contrast between the romantic view of marriage and the view endorsed by society in this story.

c How Phyllis's isolation influences her judgement.

d The effect generated by the narrator's claim that he is retelling the story Phyllis has told him.

e Why Thomas Hardy chose to have the soldiers' executed at the end of the story, rather than have them escape successfully or leave their fate unknown.

DETAILED SUMMARY

How His Cold Was Cured	Mr Stockdale is the temporary Wesleyan minister for Nether-Moynton (see Map of Wessex). On his arrival he lodges with Mrs Lizzy Newberry, a widow. He assumes Lizzy Newberry is the old woman he first meets at the house, but he later discovers that this is her mother and that Lizzy is a very attractive young woman.

Stockdale has a head cold for which Lizzy suggests brandy as a cure. She leads him to the church, where there are hidden several barrels of brandy which have been smuggled into the country. She expertly shows him how to take a draught of brandy without damaging the barrel. Stockdale is doubtful about the legitimacy of the barrel-smuggling, and is concerned about Lizzy's involvement in such activities.

Lizzy proves to be a very attentive landlady, although she sometimes stays in bed until late in the afternoon. Stockdale increasingly admires her to the point of falling in love, and she does not decline his interest in her.

How He Saw Two Other Men	One evening, about a fortnight later, Stockdale overhears a conversation between Lizzy and a man outside the house. The caller is the miller, but Stockdale also notices another man hiding in the bushes close by. Afterwards, Stockdale informs Lizzy of what he has seen. In the course of their conversation he asks her to marry him. She does not give a direct answer, but tells him she must immediately go and see her cousin Owlett, the miller, to tell him about the eavesdropper. Stockdale suspects the two have a relationship. Lizzy explains, however, that Owlett is involved in smuggling and uses her property to hide the barrels until they are collected. Stockdale disapproves of Lizzy's compliance in these matters.
The Mysterious Greatcoat	Lizzy's unusual sleeping habits give rise to some concern in Stockdale. When he questions her about it,

she replies she is not ill but sometimes does not go to sleep until very late at night. Stockdale becomes curious about her activities when a neighbour calls at the house asking for Lizzy late one night. He is unable to wake Lizzy, either by knocking on her bedroom door or by shouting loudly, and Lizzy's mother attends to the neighbour's request. Stockdale has not seen Lizzy leave the house, and her mother confirms that she is in bed, but he does not believe she could still be asleep.

Adding to his curiosity, one evening he discovers men's clothes in his room that do not belong to him; another day he sees her brushing mud off them. He questions Lizzy about this and she replies that they belong to her dead husband, and that she cleans them out of respect for his memory. Stockdale is again unconvinced, but he does not confront her about his misgivings.

At the Time of the New Moon A few nights later, Stockdale is preparing to go to bed when he hears a movement in the hallway outside his room. He looks through the door and catches a glimpse of someone who is wearing the clothes Lizzy had been brushing before. The person hurriedly disappears, and, when he realises it is Lizzy herself, Stockdale decides to follow.

Lizzy walks for three-quarters of an hour before arriving at the clifftops, whereupon she hides by a bush. Stockdale also hides when he hears the voices of a team of excise men close by. He realises that Lizzy is one of the shareholders in the smuggling, but believes that she has been forced into the venture by Owlett. Lizzy meanwhile has realised that the excise men know about the cargo about to be landed on the beach below, and she warns the boat away by setting fire to the bush.

When Lizzy returns home Stockdale reproaches her for being involved in illegal activities. Lizzy is preoccupied with saving the venture and explains how smuggling is a local tradition, and how it is not viewed so harshly by those who live in remote places. Although Stockdale strongly disapproves, he decides to follow her again in order that he might help her if something happens.

How They Went to Lulwind Cove

Lizzy leaves the house the next night, again dressed in men's clothes. Stockdale pleads with her not to go, but she is resolute. They go to Lulwind Cove (see Map of Wessex) to meet the men who will carry the barrels to a secret hiding place. They retrieve the barrels from the sea and carry them to the village. They are aware that the excise men are watching certain locations and so decide to hide some in a prepared place under an apple-tree. One of the carriers drops a barrel and it breaks open. Owlett and Lizzy are concerned about the strong smell of alcohol that will be left: a clue for the excise men.

The Great Search at Nether-Moynton

Having smelt the alcohol the previous night, Latimer, the leader of the excise team, is convinced the barrels are hidden at Nether-Moynton and he returns the next day to search the village. They arrive early, but the villagers are already prepared. Latimer and his team of thirteen Preventives systematically search the village, watched by Owlett, Lizzy and Stockdale. Latimer is determined to find the barrels but his search is in vain.

He demands the help of the locals, but to his annoyance all the men have disappeared. They are hiding in the church tower. Lizzy has heard that the excise men plan to search the church, and she goes to warn the men; a reluctant Stockdale follows her.

From their vantage point the villagers watch as the barrels hidden in the church are discovered, and then those in the orchard underneath the apple-tree. Owlett directs Lizzy to sabotage all the waggons and carts. She is not suspected by the customs team and carries out her task unnoticed.

The Walk to Warm'ell Cross and Afterwards

Latimer commandeers all of the vehicles in Nether-Moynton, but soon discovers that they are unusable since they have no linch-pins or screws; Stockdale realises Lizzy is to blame for this. Latimer also discovers that all the horses in the village have only three shoes, and the blacksmith cannot be found. The villagers' stalling tactics mean that the barrels cannot be taken away before dusk.

The villagers have planned to ambush the carts on their way to Budmouth (see Map of Wessex) and reclaim the barrels. Lizzy knows the details of the plan and goes to see what happens. Again reluctantly, Stockdale goes with her. She explains how many of the local people need the profits made through smuggling to survive.

They discover that the barrels have easily been reclaimed by the villagers, but Stockdale suspects that something terrible has happened to the excise men. He goes to look for them and discovers them tied up but uninjured. Latimer decides to give up his pursuit of the barrels.

Stockdale returns to Lizzy's house and tells her that the excise men have gone, and that he is leaving too. The subject of his final sermon is the smuggling activities that the village was involved in. He dines with Lizzy and they part on friendly terms.

Two years later Stockdale returns to Nether-Moynton. He visits Lizzy and discovers that she has given up the smuggling business. Owlett has been captured, tried and acquitted, and finally decided to emigrate to America. Lizzy's mother has died and Lizzy is very poor. She marries Stockdale and they go and live in the Midlands.

Which ending do you think is the more satisfactory?

The footnote to the story, written by Thomas Hardy thirty years later, offers a different ending – many writers earned money by serialising stories in magazines, and Thomas Hardy evidently felt some pressure from his publishers to provide an ending to the story that they would deem appropriate. In the alternative ending Lizzy remains unrepentant. She marries Owlett and they emigrate to America.

COMMENT

Thomas Hardy's choice of an **omniscient narrator** (see Literary Terms) allows him to reveal facts about characters to the reader that other characters may not be aware of. In this short story in particular it allows Thomas Hardy to present the characters and their actions in an **ironic** (see Literary Terms) way. Stockdale's continued ignorance of Lizzy's involvement in the smuggling, and then his refusal to accept her complicity in the ventures, reflect his naïve nature.

The role of religion in the village is also presented ironically as we learn that the villagers attend both the church and the chapel services, creating a 'population-puzzle' as to how 'a parish containing fifteen score of strong full-grown Episcopalians, and nearly thirteen score of well-matured Dissenters, numbered barely two-and-twenty score adults in all' (p. 86). The authorial style creates the ironic and humorous **tone** (see Literary Terms) of the story.

The setting of the story is a remote village, close to the sea. This allows Thomas Hardy to explore the superficial values of society at that time with regards to the illegal activity of smuggling (see also Themes on People and the Environment). Lizzy explains her opinions on the matter to Stockdale when he questions her about her conscience: 'My conscience is clear. I know my mother, but the king I have never seen. His dues are nothing to me. But it is a great deal to me that my mother and I should live' (p. 143).

The isolation of the villagers has created within them a set of values at odds with society, but the **irony** (see Literary Terms) and the humour in this story suggest that Thomas Hardy sympathises with the villagers. The smuggling of the barrels of brandy is presented as an adventure for Stockdale and the locals. The villagers view their brushes with the law as comical rather than serious or dangerous – in their view, the excise men are 'too stupid ever to really frighten us, and only make us a bit nimble' (p. 144).

Do you sympathise with the villagers?

The excise men are presented comically, to the extent that they are viewed as ridiculous. They are the representatives of the law and the values of society, and yet when faced with the villagers of Nether-Moynton, neither of these carries any credence. It seems that this isolated village has no respect for the law, or for the King. The customs officers' search of the village is undermined in its seriousness by the fact that they are watched by the villagers, and by the style in which it is written; it becomes increasingly ridiculous as the list of things they 'sniffed at' lengthens.

Through the romance between Stockdale and Lizzy Thomas Hardy further explores the difference in values and appropriate behaviour of upper and lower classes. Stockdale is thwarted in his attempts to elicit a promise of marriage from Lizzy as she is preoccupied by the smuggling. His concern for her leads him into compromising situations, but there is an increasing division of his loyalties: 'If I had only stuck to father's little grocery business, instead of going in for the ministry, she would have suited me beautifully!' (p. 117). He finally chooses to remain loyal to his profession and he leaves Nether-Moynton.

The ending of the story and the footnote written thirty years later illustrate the context in which Thomas Hardy was writing. It also gives us some idea about his expected readership. Because the story has raised issues of socially acceptable behaviour and loyalties to the Crown, each of the endings has a different moral overtone. The original ending reinforces society's view of appropriate behaviour through Lizzy repenting her previous disregard for the law and marrying Stockdale. The alternative ending presents Lizzy as continuing to smuggle and marrying her cousin Owlett – this could provide an altogether more subversive interpretation of the story.

GLOSSARY   **trimmers** people who alter their opinions opportunistically

viands cold meats

enkindling exciting

abstemious moderate in drinking

'nation damnation: the liquor is extremely strong

gimlet a small drill-like tool

awl a pointed tool for making holes

sampler a decorative piece of needlework made by girls to perfect and demonstrate their sewing skills

countenancing approving

backsliding becoming less virtuous, lapsing into bad habits

tutelary saints guardian or protective saints

Dissenters followers of a branch of Christianity that has separated itself from the Church of England

coquetry flirting

posset a drink made of hot milk curdled with beer or wine and flavoured with spices

expostulation strong reasoning, arguing

perfunctorily routinely, with little interest

extemporized performed without preparation

aspen trembling

grapnel small anchor

sousing plunging

mixen dung or compost heaps

casement hinged window-frame

tole entice

myrmidons unquestioning followers

Faggot-ricks stacks of bundled twigs or sticks (used as fuel)

embrasures openings

linch-pins metal pins used to hold a wheel to an axle

stoor (dialect) commotion

CHARACTERS

Richard Stockdale

Stockdale is the new preacher who is 'distracted' from carrying out his job properly because he is attracted to Lizzy Newberry. Thomas Hardy draws our attention to Stockdale's youth and inexperience, writing that Stockdale 'had scarcely as yet acquired ballast of character sufficient to steady the consciences of the hundred-and-forty Methodists of pure blood who, at this time, lived in Nether-Moynton' (p. 86). This is ominous and we expect the young minister to be overwhelmed by the villagers.

Stockdale quickly becomes party to Lizzy's involvement in smuggling. He acts impulsively when she invites him to accompany her to the secret hiding place for the brandy. He is described at this point as 'a lonely young fellow, who had for weeks felt a great craving for somebody on whom to throw away superfluous interest' (p. 91). His ingenuous reaction to the barrels highlights his lack of worldliness, and he immediately assumes that Lizzy is an unwilling participant in the smuggling.

The young minister embodies many of the prejudices of the upper classes and the church. He has a respectable background and immediately disapproves of the villagers' activities. He puts all the conventional arguments against smuggling to Lizzy, but they hold little sway in a community so isolated. On the subject of marriage he finds his loyalties divided, and only marries Lizzy when she conforms and gives up smuggling.

Thomas Hardy constructs the **plot** (see Literary Terms) around this character. His romantic interest in Lizzy leads him unwittingly and then reluctantly into the adventures of smuggling. The activities of the smugglers and the pursuit by the excise men illustrate clearly the division between the values held by society in general and the more expedient values held by the villagers. Although Stockdale compromises many of his values in his pursuit of Lizzy, he allows his values to dictate his actions and he leaves Nether-Moynton.

Lizzy
Newberry

Lizzy Newberry is a very strong female character. She is an intelligent woman whose values are determined according to her circumstances. She speaks with a 'tone of candour that was not without a touch of irony' (p. 92).

When questioned by Stockdale about the barrels, she responds evasively and he persuades himself that she is involved against her will. Lizzy uses this assumption to her own advantage. Stockdale appreciates her as an attentive landlady, whilst the reader enjoys her candid outlook on life and her sense of adventure. As the **plot** (see Literary Terms) develops she becomes more concerned about the safety of the barrels, whilst he becomes more forthright in his romantic interest in her. Lizzy's priorities are clearly with her share of the barrels as Stockdale realises that 'she had not the slightest intention of altering her plans at present' (p. 117).

Think about how other female characters in this collection of stories are subjugated by the male characters.

The extent of Lizzy's involvement in the smuggling highlights her independence, and her authority over the carriers further reinforces this. The clever and intriguing ways in which the barrels are smuggled into the country and then hidden reflect her intelligence. Along with Owlett, she easily outwits the Preventives. Her derogatory view of Latimer and his team is reinforced by the humorous accounts of their efforts to enforce the law.

Lizzy and the villagers are not totally without moral standards. When Stockdale fears for the safety of the Preventives, she exclaims: 'We don't do murder here' (p. 141). She is determined, along with the villagers, to retrieve the barrels, and to Stockdale's arguments in favour of the law she has considered replies. She cleverly finds a way of equating his behaviour with her own when she says: 'You dissent from Church, and I dissent from State' (p. 145). She is a strong-minded, resolute character for whom the values of society are to be questioned. She is surprised by the extent to which Stockdale holds on to his values, since for her, personal feelings outweigh any allegiance to Church or State.

Do you find Lizzy's change of heart plausible?

At the end of the story Lizzy is a weaker character. She has given up smuggling and repents her past involvement in it. It is this more compliant character who agrees to marry Stockdale, and he accepts her as his wife only when she conforms to the values of society. The Lizzy of the alternative ending has Thomas Hardy's endorsement, and could be seen to be more like the character presented throughout the rest of the story.

 ***Identify the speaker.***

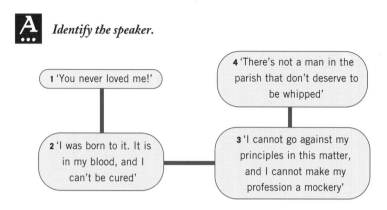

1 'You never loved me!'

4 'There's not a man in the parish that don't deserve to be whipped'

2 'I was born to it. It is in my blood, and I can't be cured'

3 'I cannot go against my principles in this matter, and I cannot make my profession a mockery'

Identify the person 'to whom' this comment refers.

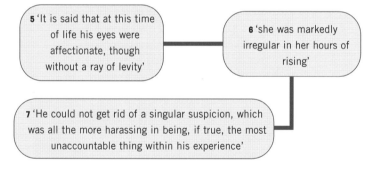

5 'It is said that at this time of life his eyes were affectionate, though without a ray of levity'

6 'she was markedly irregular in her hours of rising'

7 'He could not get rid of a singular suspicion, which was all the more harassing in being, if true, the most unaccountable thing within his experience'

Check your answers on page 89.

B ***Consider these issues.***

a To what extent Lizzy and Stockdale are similar in terms of their strength of belief.

b How the effect of the story might be different without the humorous **tone** (see Literary Terms).

c How important the setting is in exploring the values of society.

d The extra interpretations arising from the alternative ending given in the footnote.

PART THREE

COMMENTARY

THEMES

Although the short stories in *The Withered Arm and other Wessex Tales* were not originally published as one volume and are taken from different stages of Thomas Hardy's career as a writer, it is easy to identify certain themes which run through the collection as a whole, and which to some extent are representative of Thomas Hardy's thematic concerns in general.

SACRIFICE

In a number of the short stories in this collection characters are faced with dilemmas causing them to relinquish something they hold dear. The concept of sacrificing something personal is very powerful and is an effective vehicle for exploring moral and social issues.

Would there be such concerns in modern times?

In *The Son's Veto* the central character, Sophy, sacrifices her personal happiness for the benefit of her son. Randolph refuses to allow her to marry her friend Sam Hobson because of his low social status. For Randolph, such a marriage would ruin his prospects socially. It could be argued that her compliance with Randolph's wishes is the final sacrifice Sophy makes.

A refusal of marriage on Sophy's part would be perceived as an insult.

Earlier in the story she sacrifices a life of happiness when she marries Mr Twycott. Her acceptance of his offer of marriage is not based on mutual love and respect – her social status is lower than that of Mr Twycott, and she feels powerless to refuse his offer. The extent of her sacrifice in terms of personal happiness and social acceptance is emphasised throughout the story in references to her pitiable attempts to refine her behaviour and speech. After many years of marriage, Sophy still behaves and speaks in ways associated with lower social classes, and her 'great grief in this relation' is that her son feels 'irritated at their existence' (p. 40).

The theme of sacrifice in this story highlights the social divisions of the time (see Context & Setting). The only character who does not make a personal sacrifice of some sort is Randolph. He is a cruel and heartless character whose priorities lie with social acceptance rather than concern for his mother's happiness. The fact that Sophy does sacrifice her chance for personal happiness so that her son may not be impeded or embarrassed socially can be seen to be a direct criticism by Thomas Hardy of the class system and its values.

Phyllis Grove, in *The Melancholy Hussar of the German Legion*, makes a similar personal sacrifice. Again, it is the pressures of society at the time that force her to deny herself happiness instead of running away with Matthäus. She is painfully aware of the effect such an act would have and the scandal it would cause. She even convinces herself that it is her duty to honour the promise she has made to Humphrey Gould and that 'esteem must take the place of love' (p. 79).

It is ironic (see Literary Terms) that the upper-class characters do not behave honourably.

The sacrifice Phyllis makes in order to conform to social expectations highlights the power of these expectations. The fact that Humphrey Gould does not behave in a similarly honourable way could again be seen as criticism of the upper classes. In this story it is Phyllis and Matthäus who behave appropriately and who restrain their actions because they are concerned about the social consequences. Humphrey Gould's actions are driven by greed and social improvement and he does not sacrifice his chances of success in these terms. In Thomas Hardy's view, then, honourable behaviour is not to be equated with the upper classes.

Whilst the theme of sacrifice is central to these two stories, it also features to a lesser extent in other stories in this collection. Milly Richards, for example, sacrifices her self-esteem and dignity in *Tony Kytes, the Arch-Deceiver*, although in the context of the story her sacrifice can be viewed in pragmatic terms. A similar sacrifice of personal dignity can be seen in the character of Gertrude in *The Withered Arm*, who is driven by vanity to cure her arm with 'the turn o' the blood'.

PREJUDICE

The short stories in this collection explore social prejudice, and prejudice in wider terms, for example in the way characters make false assumptions, especially with regard to women.

The Son's Veto is bitter in **tone** (see Literary Terms), and it condemns the social prejudices of the upper classes. In this case, the vehicle for exposing the ugly side of such prejudices is the character of Randolph. He is the product of a class system which is divisive and judgemental. Thomas Hardy is critical of the education system which reinforces such values: at the end of the story Randolph's education has 'sufficiently ousted his humanity' and he feels justified in denying his mother her chance of happiness. Throughout the story Randolph dissociates himself from his mother, whose lower-class origins disgust him.

The contrast between the educated, cruel character of Randolph and the self-effacing character of Sophy highlights the view that such a prejudiced system is destructive in that human qualities such as happiness and forgiveness are seen as secondary to maintaining one's social status. The episode at the cricket match emphasises the superficiality of the upper classes – we see that the select society and their displays of wealth are what Randolph aspires to, and in his pursuit of this status he completely subjugates his mother.

The reaction of the squire in *Absent-mindedness in a Parish Choir* is harsh and excessive, and it is the result of his prejudiced views: he assumes that the musicians are deliberately undermining the sanctity of the church and his authority. In his opinion the musicians are uneducated people who have no understanding of how to behave appropriately. In fact, the musicians have simply made a mistake. The prejudices of the squire do not allow him to forgive the musicians, and he uses his authority to ensure they will never play in the church again.

In *The Distracted Preacher*, Richard Stockdale is prejudiced in his views about the smuggling which involves most of the villagers of Nether-Moynton. From his educated, respectable point of view the smuggling is morally and legally wrong. He cannot amend this point of view, even in the face of reasonable arguments proffered by Lizzy. At the end of the story Stockdale chooses to remain loyal to his upper-class values rather than to marry Lizzy. Even in the original ending, he only marries her once she has finally altered her opinions to conform to his point of view.

Compare Stockdale's choice to that made by Randolph in The Son's Veto.

Stockdale also makes false assumptions about Lizzy Newberry, based on the fact that she is a woman. Lizzy is a very clever, independent woman who quickly perceives a degree of naïveté in Stockdale. He presumes she is being coerced into smuggling by the men involved, but in fact, as she later admits, she finds it thrilling as well as profitable. His prejudices and his romantic involvement with Lizzy lead him to become marginally involved in the smuggling himself. He believes he should accompany Lizzy to ensure no harm comes to her. His ingenuous assumptions about Lizzy add to the humour of the story.

The prejudice of Rhoda Brook in *The Withered Arm* is against Gertrude Lodge. At the beginning of the story she is dignified in her response to the news that the father of her child has married a lady, rather than a lower-class woman like herself. Her repressed jealousy manifests itself in a dream in which she grabs Gertrude by the arm. When Rhoda finally meets Gertrude she discovers her prejudices were unfounded and her 'heart reproached her bitterly' (p. 10). Her prejudices return again at the end of the story when she discovers Gertrude laying her disfigured arm on the neck of her hanged son: 'Hussy – to come between us and our child now!'

RELATIONSHIPS

Thomas Hardy explores relationships between men and women both seriously and humorously in these short stories. The **plots** (see Literary Terms) invariably involve concerns about marriage, and through these concerns Thomas Hardy presents a fictionalised picture of society at that time (see also Context & Setting).

In *Tony Kytes, the Arch-Deceiver* the theme of relationships is examined from a humorous point of view. The predicament of Tony Kytes is that he cannot choose between the three women, each of whom suggests that she wishes to be his wife. It was expected that people would marry, and although Tony has avoided the inevitable until now, the journey home from market one day seals his fate.

The **narrator** (see Literary Terms) cannot understand why Tony is so attractive to women, and is amused by this unaccountability. The effect of this on Tony is that he treats women as simple-minded creatures to be

looked after. He would, if he could, marry all the
women in question so as not to hurt any of their
feelings. The sequence of events leading up to the
climax (see Literary Terms) of the story – the
confrontation in the road – is almost farcical, with the
ending emphasising the fact that in the long run, no
real harm has been done.

The women in this story all behave in extraordinary
ways. Milly Richards is possibly the least reprehensible,
although she is, like Unity Sallet, gullible enough to
demean herself by hiding in the waggon at Tony's
request. Unity Sallet and Hannah Jolliver are both
flirtatious women who try to persuade Tony that they
would make him a better wife than Milly would.

Tony Kytes
instantly rejects
his father's advice.

Tony seeks advice from his father, who declares that
Milly will be the better wife because she did not
ask to ride with Tony. Tony's reaction to this
recommendation is to ask Hannah Jolliver to marry
him – parental approval of a future spouse is a blow to
Milly's prospects. Tony finally declares to Milly that 'it
do seem as if fate had ordained that it should be you
and I, or nobody.' She accepts him as her husband;
perhaps a pragmatic and sensible action in the long run.

Stockdale's pursuit of Lizzy in *The Distracted Preacher* is
also presented comically. His assumptions about Lizzy
are proved wrong as he finds himself in increasingly
compromising situations with regard to the smuggling.
There is also a serious side to their relationship which
concerns Stockdale's social values and beliefs. He is
adamant that he cannot marry her whilst she will not
accept that smuggling is wrong. Lizzy, in turn, is
adamant that they are 'well matched', both dissenters in
their own ways.

The lack of forgiveness and warmth evident in
Stockdale's departure, choosing to maintain his social

status rather than marry Lizzy, shows how relationships
at the time were complicated by concerns other than
personal feelings. In other short stories in this collection
marriages, engagements and relationships seem to be
governed by external rather than personal concerns.

In *The Son's Veto* Sophy is too overawed to refuse
Mr Twycott's offer of marriage. Her lack of self-esteem
leads her into a life of self-effacement and constantly
feeling inadequate. Their marriage satisfies Twycott's
need for companionship even though he 'knew perfectly
well that he had committed social suicide' (p. 39) in
marrying Sophy. The prospect of personal happiness for
Sophy is to marry Sam and lead 'an idyllic life with her
faithful fruiterer and greengrocer' (p. 50), but Randolph
forbids this. In Sophy's case it is not her own social
aspirations, but her son's, that prevent her marrying the
man she loves.

Phyllis Grove and Sophy Twycott are both presented as victims of society.

Phyllis Grove, in *The Melancholy Hussar of the German
Legion*, is similarly a victim of society in that she
chooses to behave in a way which does not compromise
herself or her father in the eyes of society. Unhappily
for her, other characters are less than scrupulous in their
behaviour. Humphrey Gould, to whom she is engaged,
views marriage as a means of improving his social and
financial status, and ultimately he does not honour his
promise of marriage to Phyllis.

Social pressures treat Phyllis cruelly. She and Matthäus
do behave honourably towards each other, but their
marriage would be untenable in the eyes of society. She
decides to martyr herself to social conformity: 'She
would stay at home, and marry him, and suffer' (p. 79).
When she discovers she has been misled by Humphrey,
it is too late for her to leave with Matthäus.

The marriage of Farmer Lodge in *The Withered Arm* is
not in itself reprehensible, although the reader quickly

learns that he has had a previous relationship with a woman of a lower social class: Rhoda Brook. Marriages between people of different social classes were frowned upon by society, and Farmer Lodge chooses a more appropriate wife, a 'lady complete'. The poverty in which Rhoda and their son live, completely ignored by Farmer Lodge, is compensated for by the mysterious injury to Gertrude Lodge's arm which ruins their marriage. Farmer Lodge himself fears the injury might be 'a judgement from heaven upon him' (p. 19). Again, social concerns have complicated the choice of a spouse with disastrous consequences.

MORAL STANDARDS

Thomas Hardy exposes the divide between the perceived moral standards of the upper classes and the ways in which people behave in reality. The lower classes were considered to be virtually uncivilised, but in these short stories they behave more reasonably and with more forgiveness than the upper classes.

In *The Withered Arm* Rhoda has been rejected by Farmer Lodge and left to live a life of poverty as an outcast. He completely ignores Rhoda and their son, although they live close by, and he denies knowing his son to his new wife Gertrude. In contrast to his behaviour, Rhoda maintains a pragmatic view of life and refuses to join in with the gossip about his new wife. She feels some pity for Gertrude when she learns about the mysterious affliction, and even feels that she is responsible for the injury. It is not until the end of the story that Farmer Lodge 'changed for the better, and appeared as a chastened and thoughtful man' (p. 32).

Thomas Hardy's most embittered attack on the moral standards of the upper classes is *The Son's Veto*. The character of Randolph is presented as harsh in the extreme, influenced by wealth and the superficial values of the select upper classes. It is **ironic** (see Literary Terms) that the most uncharitable and unforgiving character in the story becomes a minister for the Church, supposedly to direct society as to the correct way to behave.

The outrageous way in which Randolph behaves is emphasised by the contrast between him and Sophy. She would not do anything to upset her son or damage his prospects. He is relentless in his chastisement of his mother, and she pays the ultimate price, dying in sadness when she could have been happily married to Sam 'and nobody have been anything the worse in the world' (p. 50). The destructive nature of the values fervently adhered to by Randolph is evident.

The moral standards of the inhabitants of Nether-Moynton are in question according to Richard Stockdale in *The Distracted Preacher*. Thomas Hardy presents their smuggling in humorous terms, and their behaviour is seen to be expedient rather than immoral. The fact that Stockdale adheres to his values at the expense of marrying Lizzy is evidence that the moral standards expected by society govern his judgement, rather than his personal feelings.

PEOPLE AND THE ENVIRONMENT

Many of the themes discussed are developed in relation to people and their environment; the characters in these short stories are influenced by their environment either positively or negatively. The moral standards of civilised society (see above) are perceived differently in the remote settings of these stories, and class divisions are more pronounced.

In the stories set in remote communities, Thomas Hardy uses the environment to develop his themes. Stockdale's civilised values are constantly called into question in *The Distracted Preacher*, as in this community these values appear to be less pertinent to the villagers than the use of their isolation to their best advantage. In *The Withered Arm* the small size of the community makes it inevitable that Rhoda and Gertrude will meet. The superstitions of the community take on a more sinister aspect as the locals believe Rhoda to be the cause of Gertrude's affliction.

In *The Melancholy Hussar of the German Legion* the isolation of the community again plays its part. Marriage prospects are few for Phyllis and it is seen as a triumph for her when she becomes engaged to Humphrey Gould. He leaves to visit the large community of Bath; very little is heard of him and she is attracted to the romantic figure of Matthäus. Her vulnerability is emphasised through her isolation.

Social status and appropriate behaviour acquire more relevance in a small community in which it is difficult to be discreet. These concerns are evident in Phyllis's behaviour in *The Melancholy Hussar of the German Legion*, and in the excessive actions of the squire in *Absent-mindedness in a Parish Choir*. In *The Distracted Preacher* Stockdale finds his position increasingly compromised through his association with the smugglers, who of course all recognise him as the local minister. Even in *Tony Kytes, the Arch-Deceiver* the disapproving voice of Tony's father reflects the importance of being seen to behave appropriately instead of 'driving about the country with Jolliver's daughter and making a scandal' (p. 57).

STRUCTURE

The structural features of a short story are different to those of other prose fiction. Short stories are often **anecdotal**, with all of the events leading to a swift and dramatic conclusion or **dénouement** (see Literary Terms).

LENGTH

The length of the short stories in this collection varies greatly. *The Withered Arm* and *The Distracted Preacher* are the longest with the most complex **plots**. The events in *The Withered Arm* focus upon the two women characters and Gertrude's desperation to receive 'the cure'. The dramatic **climax** (see Literary Terms) of this story is carefully preceded by Gertrude's elaborate preparations to attend the hanging. The shortest stories are the humorous ones; these have the sense of a friend recounting a funny story.

CHARACTERS

Short stories tend to focus on two or three **characters** (see Literary Terms), although there may be peripheral characters in them as well. In novels, characters can be developed at length, whereas in short stories they have to be established swiftly. Because of this, they often have a predominant trait or quality, rather than being more 'rounded' characters backed up with detailed descriptions. In *The Son's Veto*, for example, the character of Randolph primarily embodies the superficiality and lack of morals of the upper classes, whereas the character of Sam serves to bring concern and warmth to the story.

TWIST IN THE TALE

To create a sense of completeness or **closure** (see Literary Terms) the endings of short stories often have a 'twist in the tale', or a surprising ending. In

The Withered Arm the ending is dramatic and shocking; in *Tony Kytes, the Arch-Deceiver* the events culminate in humiliation for most of the characters. The endings of *The Son's Veto* and *The Melancholy Hussar of the German Legion* are more poignant because of the **objective** perspective adopted by the **narrator** (see Literary Terms) in each case.

TIME SPAN

The time span of short stories tends to be limited, often focusing on a single incident or idea. In these short stories the time spans vary from a single afternoon to several years. The events given significance in stories with a long time span focus upon one character or idea: for example, the deteriorating condition of Gertrude's arm is the dominant idea in *The Withered Arm*, and the long time span of the story allows this to be developed. By contrast, the unfortunate events of a single church service are the focus for *Absent-mindedness in a Parish Choir*. The very short time span of this story emphasises the extremity of the musicians' 'punishment' – never to play in the church again.

LANGUAGE & STYLE

Short stories rely on **dialogue** and description to carry the **plot** (see Literary Terms) forward swiftly. Thomas Hardy uses a variety of styles of **narrative** which, combined with the dialogue and description, establish the **tone** (see Literary Terms) of the stories. His use of regional dialect in the stories tends to identify the social class of the characters.

NARRATIVE STYLES

Thomas Hardy uses **first-person narrators** (see Literary Terms) who speak with a regional dialect for his humorous stories. This style of narration immediately establishes an informal tone and the use of a regional dialect creates a friendly atmosphere for the **anecdote** (see Literary Terms). The **omniscient** (see Literary Terms) style of narration is used in the more serious stories in which Thomas Hardy is exploring issues of social division and morality.

Thomas Hardy relies on the lack of pretension associated with regional dialects, and it is the uneducated, lower-class characters who speak with a regional dialect in the stories. The more formal Standard English is used by the upper-class characters, and signifies their conformity with social standards of behaviour. The irritation of Randolph in *The Son's Veto* at his mother's use of a regional dialect reflects the superficiality of these standards.

DESCRIPTION

Through his descriptions Thomas Hardy develops our understanding of the characters. A character's physical appearance can indicate their nature, whilst their clothes can help to establish their social status. The characters' homes often reflect their state of mind or their situation. This is especially evident in *The Son's Veto* when the comfortable home in Gaymead is abandoned for a 'narrow, dusty house in a long, straight street' (p. 39). In *The Withered Arm* Rhoda's home is remote from the village, a fact which suggests her status as an outcast. The sturdy walls have endured harsh treatment from the weather, and perhaps reflect how Rhoda has passively suffered Lodge's rejection. At the start of the story Rhoda is described as 'the thin worn milkmaid' (p. 2). This economy of style is continued with the **simile** (see Literary Terms) of the rafter showing through the thatch: 'like a bone protruding through the skin' (p. 3). Thomas Hardy has created an image of a shabby cottage in a state of disrepair, whilst at the same time enhancing our view of Rhoda as a woman of haggard appearance.

DIALOGUE

The dialogue in the stories allows us to identify the relationships between the characters. The distance between Sophy and Randolph is evident in *The Son's Veto*, as is the genuine affection of Sam. Randolph's initial admonishment of his mother (*'Has*, dear mother – not *have*!'*, p. 36) illustrates his concern about social correctness and his anger that his mother is socially inferior to his circle of friends.

In *The Distracted Preacher* we can discern the evasiveness of Lizzy's responses to Stockdale's questions, which establish her superiority. When Stockdale asks her about the barrels she replies 'I cannot inform, in fact, against anybody' (p. 94), and the reader immediately suspects her personal involvement in the smuggling.

The dialogue in *Tony Kytes, the Arch-Deceiver* adds to the humour of the story because of its context, as when Tony is trying to respond to the advances of Hannah whilst Milly and Unity are within earshot (hiding in the waggon). He denies he is engaged to Milly, but he speaks quietly since Milly is close by under the tarpaulin (p. 55):

' "You've settled it with Milly by this time, I suppose," said she.

' "N–no, not exactly."

' "What? How low you talk, Tony."

' "Yes – I've a kind of hoarseness. I said, not exactly."

He gives further excuses as Hannah hears Milly's squeaks from under the tarpaulin, and his desperation becomes evident: 'And – and – what a fine day it is, isn't it, Hannah, for this time of year? Be you going to market next Saturday? How is your aunt now?' (p. 56).

PART FOUR

STUDY SKILLS

HOW TO USE QUOTATIONS

One of the secrets of success in writing essays is the way you use quotations. There are five basic principles:

- Put inverted commas at the beginning and end of the quotation
- Write the quotation exactly as it appears in the original
- Do not use a quotation that repeats what you have just written
- Use the quotation so that it fits into your sentence
- Keep the quotation as short as possible

Quotations should be used to develop the line of thought in your essays.

Your comment should not duplicate what is in your quotation. For example:

> Matthäus could have tried to persuade Phyllis to come with him, but he does not try to convince her forcefully: 'But he did nothing to tempt her unduly or unfairly.'

Far more effective is to write:

> Matthäus could have tried to persuade Phyllis to come with him, 'But he did nothing to tempt her unduly or unfairly.'

However, the most sophisticated way of using the writer's words is to embed them into your sentence:

> Although she has not yet seen the much-talked-about 'lady complete', Rhoda is able to form a mental picture of Farmer Lodge's new wife that is 'realistic as a photograph'.

When you use quotations in this way, you are demonstrating the ability to use text as evidence to support your ideas – not simply including words from the original to prove you have read it.

Everyone writes differently. Work through the suggestions given here and adapt the advice to suit your own style and interests. This will improve your essay-writing skills and allow your personal voice to emerge.

The following points indicate in ascending order the skills of essay writing:

- Picking out one or two facts about the story and adding the odd detail
- Writing about the text by retelling the story
- Retelling the story and adding a quotation here and there
- Organising an answer which explains what is happening in the text and giving quotations to support what you write

....

- Writing in such a way as to show that you have thought about the intentions of the writer of the text and that you understand the techniques used
- Writing at some length, giving your viewpoint on the text and commenting by picking out details to support your views
- Looking at the text as a work of art, demonstrating clear critical judgement and explaining to the reader of your essay how the enjoyment of the text is assisted by literary devices, linguistic effects and psychological insights; showing how the text relates to the time when it was written

The dotted line above represents the division between lower- and higher-level grades. Higher-level performance begins when you start to consider your response as a reader of the text. The highest level is reached when you offer an enthusiastic personal response and show how this piece of literature is a product of its time.

Coursework essay

Set aside an hour or so at the start of your work to plan what you have to do.

- List all the points you feel are needed to cover the task. Collect page references of information and quotations that will support what you have to say. A helpful tool is the highlighter pen: this saves painstaking copying and enables you to target precisely what you want to use.
- Focus on what you consider to be the main points of the essay. Try to sum up your argument in a single sentence, which could be the closing sentence of your essay. Depending on the essay title, it could be a statement about a character: At the end of *The Son's Veto*, even after his mother's death, Randolph remains aloof and arrogant; an opinion about a setting: The isolation of the hamlet in *The Melancholy Hussar of the German Legion* contributes to Phyllis's inexperience and vulnerability; or a judgement on a theme: The theme of sacrifice is poignantly explored in *The Son's Veto* through the irreconcilable demands of society's conventions and Sophy's personal happiness.
- Make a short essay plan. Use the first paragraph to introduce the argument you wish to make. In the following paragraphs develop this argument with details, examples and other possible points of view. Sum up your argument in the last paragraph. Check you have answered the question.
- Write the essay, remembering all the time the central point you are making.
- On completion, go back over what you have written to eliminate careless errors and improve expression. Read it aloud to yourself, or, if you are feeling more confident, to a relative or friend.

If you can, try to type your essay, using a word processor. This will allow you to correct and improve your writing without spoiling its appearance.

Examination essay

The essay written in an examination often carries more marks than the coursework essay even though it is written under considerable time pressure.

In the revision period build up notes on various aspects of the text you are using. Fortunately, in acquiring this set of York Notes on *The Withered Arm and other Wessex Tales*, you have made a prudent beginning! York Notes are set out to give you vital information and help you to construct your personal overview of the text.

Make notes with appropriate quotations about the key issues of the set text. Go into the examination knowing your text and having a clear set of opinions about it.

In most English Literature examinations you can take in copies of your set books. This is an enormous advantage although it may lull you into a false sense of security. Beware! There is simply not enough time in an examination to read the book from scratch.

In the examination

- Read the question paper carefully and remind yourself what you have to do.
- Look at the questions on your set texts to select the one that most interests you and mentally work out the points you wish to stress.
- Remind yourself of the time available and how you are going to use it.
- Briefly map out a short plan in note form that will keep your writing on track and illustrate the key argument you want to make.
- Then set about writing it.
- When you have finished, check through to eliminate errors.

To summarise, these are the keys to success:

- **Know the text**
- **Have a clear understanding of and opinions on the storyline, characters, setting, themes and writer's concerns**
- **Select the right material**
- **Plan and write a clear response, continually bearing the question in mind**

A typical essay question on *The Withered Arm and other Wessex Tales* is followed by a sample essay plan in note form. This does not present the only answer to the question, merely one answer. Do not be afraid to include your own ideas and leave out some of the ones in this sample! Remember that quotations are essential to prove and illustrate the points you make.

Discuss how Thomas Hardy presents concerns about marriage in two of the short stories from this collection.

Preparation   Think about how you could group the stories. Are any of them similar in their presentation of men and women? Try to take an overview, with a view to drawing comparisons and highlighting contrasts between the stories.

Introduction   General comment about how many characters in the collection face difficulties/dilemmas about marriage. Briefly outline the context of the stories – class system, rural England, etc. (use Context & Setting as starting point). Look at the social implications of marriage and how they are explored (e.g. in *The Son's Veto* and *The Distracted Preacher*).

The Son's Veto   Effect of Sophy's marriage to Twycott. Explain what typifies the relationship between Randolph and his mother. Describe her life, both before and after Twycott's death.

Why does she start thinking about her life in Gaymead when she is widowed? What effect does the reappearance of Sam Hobson have upon Sophy? Explain why she needs Randolph's approval before she will marry Sam. Consider what the social implications of her marrying Sam would be both for herself and for Randolph.

Comment on the ending. What effect does Thomas Hardy achieve by using a bitter **tone**? How does it make us view the class system?

The Distracted Preacher

Describe Stockdale's introduction at the beginning of the story and how Lizzy introduces him to the world of smuggling. Contrast the humorous style with *The Son's Veto*. What is Stockdale's initial opinion of Lizzy? What are her first impressions of him?

Explain the arguments he uses to persuade her to give up smuggling. What is her reaction to these arguments?

Why does Stockdale decide he cannot marry Lizzy? Comment on her reaction to his decision to leave Nether-Moynton.

How has Lizzy changed by the end of the story? Why does Stockdale decide he can now marry her? Describe the alternative ending and explain which you find to be more satisfactory and why. What does Thomas Hardy present as the major concerns when it comes to choosing a husband/wife in this story?

Conclusion

The dilemmas about marriage are resolved in different ways in each of these short stories; but explain what they have in common. What do the women characters sacrifice in these stories? Explain what kind of comment you think Thomas Hardy is making about the Victorian class system.

FURTHER QUESTIONS

Make a plan as shown above and attempt these questions:

1 Discuss the importance of the setting in three of the stories in this collection.
2 How does Thomas Hardy present upper-class characters in these stories?

3 The historical context of these stories is dominated by class divisions. Discuss how Thomas Hardy explores the effects of these divisions in three stories from this collection.

4 Compare and contrast the characters of Phyllis in *The Melancholy Hussar of the German Legion* and Sophy in *The Son's Veto*.

5 Explore the religious characters' lack of humility in two of the stories.

6 Discuss the importance of marriage in the short stories.

7 To what extent does Thomas Hardy show the moral standards of society to be superficial in these stories?

8 Explore the theme of sacrifice in two of the short stories in this collection.

9 Consider the effects generated by the two different endings to *The Distracted Preacher*.

10 Both Randolph in *The Son's Veto* and Stockdale in *The Distracted Preacher* refuse to compromise their upper-class values. How are our reactions to these characters affected by the different narrative **tones** used in the two stories?

PART FIVE

CULTURAL CONNECTIONS

BROADER PERSPECTIVES

Similar themes to those found in *The Withered Arm and other Wessex Tales* are also explored in Thomas Hardy's *Tess of the d'Urbervilles* and *Far from the Madding Crowd*. Both of these novels examine issues of marriage and social expectations.

Other writers who explore social concerns include George Eliot in *Silas Marner* and Charles Dickens in *Hard Times* and *Bleak House*. In particular, these stories deal with inequalities in the class system and their effects on both individuals and society. The theme of social prejudice is examined in different ways in *To Kill a Mockingbird* by Harper Lee and *Roll of Thunder, Hear My Cry* by Mildred D. Taylor.

Milly Richards in *Tony Kytes, the Arch-Deceiver* can be compared to Dorothea in Kate Chopin's story *The Unexpected*, which can be found in *The New Windmill Book of Nineteenth Century Short Stories* (Heinemann, 1992). Both stories explore relationships and social conventions. Relationships between men and women are also the subject of *Tickets Please*, a short story by D.H. Lawrence.

Roald Dahl's short story collections *The Great Automatic Grammatizator and Other Stories* and *Tales of the Unexpected* make varied use of the 'twist in the tale' structure.

Nightmares and Dreamscapes, a collection of short stories by Stephen King, and *The Turn of the Screw*, a short story by Henry James, all include aspects of the supernatural as found in *The Withered Arm*.

anecdote a narrative of an interesting sequence of small events and incidents, usually intended to be entertaining or humorous

character an invented, imaginary person in a work of literature (though characters may be based on real people), with human qualities and behaviour

climax the culmination of a sequence of events in a narrative

closure the sense of completeness or finality achieved by the ending of a literary work, for example when Rhoda returns to her village at the end of *The Withered Arm* and the reader feels that the story has 'come full circle'

dénouement (French: 'unknotting') the final unfolding of a plot: the point at which the reader's expectations about what will happen to the characters are finally satisfied or denied

dialogue the speech and conversation of characters in a work of literature

didactic intended to instruct or persuade

empathy the effect of mentally identifying with a character in a story, to the point of fully understanding his or her thoughts, feelings and actions

first-person narrative a story told from the point of view of an 'I' figure, directly involved in the action

flashback a sudden jump backwards in time to an earlier episode or incident

irony a use of language in which a speaker or writer states one thing but means something else. Words spoken innocently but which later prove to be mistaken or to have prophesied an event are also termed 'ironic'

microcosm a miniature representation of something. For example, although the stories in *The Withered Arm and other Wessex Tales* are mostly set in very small rural communities, they are intended to be representative of English society in general

narrative a story, tale or recital of a specific selection of events

narrator the person who tells the story. The narrator can be distinguished from the author of a work, and can in some senses be thought of as another character. In *Tony Kytes, the Arch-Deceiver*, for example, although we know that Thomas Hardy is the author of the story, we imagine the narrator to be someone else, telling the story to a friend

objective written in a detached and matter-of-fact style, rather than in a personal and emotionally involved way

omniscient narrator a storyteller with total knowledge of characters' thoughts, feelings and actions

parallel an establishing of similarities between characters or events in a work of literature

pathos a strong feeling of pity or sorrow

plot the sequence of events in a story and the various relationships between these events

simile a direct comparison of one thing to another. For example, when Phyllis witnesses the execution of the two soldiers in *The Melancholy Hussar of the German Legion*, Thomas Hardy writes of 'her face as if hardened to stone' (p. 83)

suspense the state of uncertainty and curiosity brought about by delaying the climax of a narrative, as the reader wants to find out what will happen

symbol an object or idea which is used to represent something else

sympathy the reader's recognition of the feelings of a character

theme a central idea explored in a text

tone the mood or manner in which a text is intended to be read

(The Withered Arm)

A 1 Rhoda Brook *(p. 31)*
··· 2 Farmer Lodge *(p. 19)*
   3 Gertrude Lodge *(p. 28)*
   4 Rhoda's son *(p. 5)*
   5 Conjuror Trendle *(p. 16)*
   6 Rhoda Brook *(p. 14)*
   7 Gertrude Lodge *(p. 7)*

Test yourself
(The Son's Veto)

A 1 Sam Hobson *(p. 47)*
··· 2 Randolph *(p. 49)*
   3 Sophy *(p. 47)*
   4 Sophy and Mr Twycott *(p. 39)*
   5 Sam Hobson *(p. 50)*
   6 Randolph *(p. 50)*

Test yourself
(Tony Kytes, the Arch-Deceiver)

A 1 Unity Sallet *(p. 52)*
··· 2 Milly Richards *(p. 58)*
   3 Tony Kytes *(p. 59)*
   4 Hannah Jolliver *(p. 60)*
   5 Tony Kytes *(p. 55)*
   6 Milly Richards *(p. 58)*
   7 Hannah Jolliver *(p. 53)*

Test yourself
(Absent-mindedness in a Parish Choir)

A 1 Nicholas Puddingcome *(pp. 61–2)*
··· 2 The squire *(p. 63)*
   3 The squire *(p. 64)*
   4 The musicians *(p. 62)*

Test yourself
(The Melancholy Hussar of the German Legion)

A 1 Dr Grove *(p. 73)*
··· 2 Matthäus Tina *(p. 74)*
   3 Phyllis Grove *(p. 73)*
   4 Humphrey Gould *(p. 78)*
   5 Matthäus Tina *(p. 79)*
   6 Humphrey Gould *(p. 72)*

Test yourself
(The Distracted Preacher)

A 1 Lizzy *(p. 145)*
··· 2 Lizzy *(p. 144)*
   3 Stockdale *(p. 144)*
   4 Latimer *(p. 137)*
   5 Stockdale *(p. 86)*
   6 Lizzy *(p. 102)*
   7 Stockdale *(p. 105)*

Notes

GCSE and equivalent levels (£3.50 each)

Maya Angelou
I Know Why the Caged Bird Sings

Jane Austen
Pride and Prejudice

Alan Ayckbourn
Absent Friends

Elizabeth Barrett Browning
Selected Poems

Robert Bolt
A Man for All Seasons

Harold Brighouse
Hobson's Choice

Charlotte Brontë
Jane Eyre

Emily Brontë
Wuthering Heights

Shelagh Delaney
A Taste of Honey

Charles Dickens
David Copperfield

Charles Dickens
Great Expectations

Charles Dickens
Hard Times

Charles Dickens
Oliver Twist

Roddy Doyle
Paddy Clarke Ha Ha Ha

George Eliot
Silas Marner

George Eliot
The Mill on the Floss

William Golding
Lord of the Flies

Oliver Goldsmith
She Stoops To Conquer

Willis Hall
The Long and the Short and the Tall

Thomas Hardy
Far from the Madding Crowd

Thomas Hardy
The Mayor of Casterbridge

Thomas Hardy
Tess of the d'Urbervilles

Thomas Hardy
The Withered Arm and other Wessex Tales

L.P. Hartley
The Go-Between

Seamus Heaney
Selected Poems

Susan Hill
I'm the King of the Castle

Barry Hines
A Kestrel for a Knave

Louise Lawrence
Children of the Dust

Harper Lee
To Kill a Mockingbird

Laurie Lee
Cider with Rosie

Arthur Miller
The Crucible

Arthur Miller
A View from the Bridge

Robert O'Brien
Z for Zachariah

Frank O'Connor
My Oedipus Complex and other stories

George Orwell
Animal Farm

J.B. Priestley
An Inspector Calls

Willy Russell
Educating Rita

Willy Russell
Our Day Out

J.D. Salinger
The Catcher in the Rye

William Shakespeare
Henry IV Part 1

William Shakespeare
Henry V

William Shakespeare
Julius Caesar

William Shakespeare
Macbeth

William Shakespeare
The Merchant of Venice

William Shakespeare
A Midsummer Night's Dream

William Shakespeare
Much Ado About Nothing

William Shakespeare
Romeo and Juliet

William Shakespeare
The Tempest

William Shakespeare
Twelfth Night

George Bernard Shaw
Pygmalion

Mary Shelley
Frankenstein

R.C. Sherriff
Journey's End

Rukshana Smith
Salt on the snow

John Steinbeck
Of Mice and Men

Robert Louis Stevenson
Dr Jekyll and Mr Hyde

Jonathan Swift
Gulliver's Travels

Robert Swindells
Daz 4 Zoe

Mildred D. Taylor
Roll of Thunder, Hear My Cry

Mark Twain
Huckleberry Finn

James Watson
Talking in Whispers

William Wordsworth
Selected Poems

A Choice of Poets

Mystery Stories of the Nineteenth Century including The Signalman

Nineteenth Century Short Stories

Poetry of the First World War

Six Women Poets

York Notes Advanced (£3.99 each)

Margaret Atwood
The Handmaid's Tale

Jane Austen
Mansfield Park

Jane Austen
Persuasion

Jane Austen
Pride and Prejudice

Alan Bennett
Talking Heads

William Blake
Songs of Innocence and of Experience

Charlotte Brontë
Jane Eyre

Emily Brontë
Wuthering Heights

Geoffrey Chaucer
The Franklin's Tale

Geoffrey Chaucer
General Prologue to the Canterbury Tales

Geoffrey Chaucer
The Wife of Bath's Prologue and Tale

Joseph Conrad
Heart of Darkness

Charles Dickens
Great Expectations

John Donne
Selected Poems

George Eliot
The Mill on the Floss

F. Scott Fitzgerald
The Great Gatsby

E.M. Forster
A Passage to India

Brian Friel
Translations

Thomas Hardy
The Mayor of Casterbridge

Thomas Hardy
Tess of the d'Urbervilles

Seamus Heaney
Selected Poems from Opened Ground

Nathaniel Hawthorne
The Scarlet Letter

James Joyce
Dubliners

John Keats
Selected Poems

Christopher Marlowe
Doctor Faustus

Arthur Miller
Death of a Salesman

Toni Morrison
Beloved

William Shakespeare
Antony and Cleopatra

William Shakespeare
As You Like It

William Shakespeare
Hamlet

William Shakespeare
King Lear

William Shakespeare
Measure for Measure

William Shakespeare
The Merchant of Venice

William Shakespeare
Much Ado About Nothing

William Shakespeare
Othello

William Shakespeare
Romeo and Juliet

William Shakespeare
The Tempest

William Shakespeare
The Winter's Tale

Mary Shelley
Frankenstein

Alice Walker
The Color Purple

Oscar Wilde
The Importance of Being Earnest

Tennessee Williams
A Streetcar Named Desire

John Webster
The Duchess of Malfi

W.B. Yeats
Selected Poems

Chinua Achebe
Things Fall Apart

Edward Albee
Who's Afraid of Virginia Woolf?

Margaret Atwood
Cat's Eye

Jane Austen
Emma

Jane Austen
Northanger Abbey

Jane Austen
Sense and Sensibility

Samuel Beckett
Waiting for Godot

Robert Browning
Selected Poems

Robert Burns
Selected Poems

Angela Carter
Nights at the Circus

Geoffrey Chaucer
The Merchant's Tale

Geoffrey Chaucer
The Miller's Tale

Geoffrey Chaucer
The Nun's Priest's Tale

Samuel Taylor Coleridge
Selected Poems

Daniel Defoe
Moll Flanders

Daniel Defoe
Robinson Crusoe

Charles Dickens
Bleak House

Charles Dickens
Hard Times

Emily Dickinson
Selected Poems

Carol Ann Duffy
Selected Poems

George Eliot
Middlemarch

T.S. Eliot
The Waste Land

T.S. Eliot
Selected Poems

Henry Fielding
Joseph Andrews

E.M. Forster
Howards End

John Fowles
The French Lieutenant's Woman

Robert Frost
Selected Poems

Elizabeth Gaskell
North and South

Stella Gibbons
Cold Comfort Farm

Graham Greene
Brighton Rock

Thomas Hardy
Jude the Obscure

Thomas Hardy
Selected Poems

Joseph Heller
Catch-22

Homer
The Iliad

Homer
The Odyssey

Gerard Manley Hopkins
Selected Poems

Aldous Huxley
Brave New World

Kazuo Ishiguro
The Remains of the Day

Ben Jonson
The Alchemist

Ben Jonson
Volpone

James Joyce
A Portrait of the Artist as a Young Man

Philip Larkin
Selected Poems

D.H. Lawrence
The Rainbow

D.H. Lawrence
Selected Stories

D.H. Lawrence
Sons and Lovers

D.H. Lawrence
Women in Love

John Milton
Paradise Lost Bks I & II

John Milton
Paradise Lost Bks IV & IX

Thomas More
Utopia

Sean O'Casey
Juno and the Paycock

George Orwell
Nineteen Eighty-four

John Osborne
Look Back in Anger

Wilfred Owen
Selected Poems

Sylvia Plath
Selected Poems

Alexander Pope
Rape of the Lock and other poems

Ruth Prawer Jhabvala
Heat and Dust

Jean Rhys
Wide Sargasso Sea

William Shakespeare
As You Like It

William Shakespeare
Coriolanus

William Shakespeare
Henry IV Pt 1

William Shakespeare
Henry V

William Shakespeare
Julius Caesar

William Shakespeare
Macbeth

William Shakespeare
Measure for Measure

William Shakespeare
A Midsummer Night's Dream

William Shakespeare
Richard II

William Shakespeare
Richard III

William Shakespeare
Sonnets

William Shakespeare
The Taming of the Shrew

William Shakespeare
Twelfth Night

William Shakespeare
The Winter's Tale

George Bernard Shaw
Arms and the Man

George Bernard Shaw
Saint Joan

Muriel Spark
The Prime of Miss Jean Brodie

John Steinbeck
The Grapes of Wrath

John Steinbeck
The Pearl

Tom Stoppard
Arcadia

Tom Stoppard
*Rosencrantz and Guildenstern
are Dead*

Jonathan Swift
*Gulliver's Travels and The
Modest Proposal*

Alfred, Lord Tennyson
Selected Poems

W.M. Thackeray
Vanity Fair

Virgil
The Aeneid

Edith Wharton
The Age of Innocence

Tennessee Williams
Cat on a Hot Tin Roof

Tennessee Williams
The Glass Menagerie

Virginia Woolf
Mrs Dalloway

Virginia Woolf
To the Lighthouse

William Wordsworth
Selected Poems

Metaphysical Poets

York Notes – the Ultimate Literature Guides

York Notes are recognised as the best literature study guides.
If you have enjoyed using this book and have found it useful, you
can now order others directly from us – simply follow the ordering
instructions below.

HOW TO ORDER

Decide which title(s) you require and then order in one of the following
ways:

Booksellers
All titles available from good bookstores.

By post
List the title(s) you require in the space provided overleaf,
select your method of payment, complete your name and
address details and return your completed order form and
payment to:

> *Addison Wesley Longman Ltd*
> *PO BOX 88*
> *Harlow*
> *Essex CM19 5SR*

By phone
Call our Customer Information Centre on 01279 623923 to
place your order, quoting mail number: HEYN1.

By fax
Complete the order form overleaf, ensuring you fill in your
name and address details and method of payment, and fax it
to us on 01279 414130.

By e-mail
E-mail your order to us on awlhe.orders@awl.co.uk listing
title(s) and quantity required and providing full name and
address details as requested overleaf. Please quote mail
number: HEYN1. Please do not send credit card details by
e-mail.

York Notes Order Form

Titles required:

Quantity	Title/ISBN	Price

Sub total _____

Please add £2.50 postage & packing _____

(*P & P is free for orders over £50*) _____

Total _____

Mail no: HEYN1

Your Name _____

Your Address _____

Postcode _____ Telephone _____

Method of payment

☐ I enclose a cheque or a P/O for £_____ made payable to Addison Wesley Longman Ltd

☐ Please charge my Visa/Access/AMEX/Diners Club card

Number _____ Expiry Date _____

Signature _____ Date _____

(please ensure that the address given above is the same as for your credit card)

Prices and other details are correct at time of going to press but may change without notice. All orders are subject to status.

☐ *Please tick this box if you would like a complete listing of Longman Study Guides (suitable for GCSE and A-level students)*

York Press

Longman

Addison Wesley Longman